Anglers' Paradise

FAVOURITE NEW ZEALAND FISHING WATERS
AND THE FLIES TO FISH THEM WITH

Anglers' Paradise

FAVOURITE FISHING WATERS OF NEW ZEALAND
AND THE FLIES TO FISH THEM WITH

Illustrated by Nancy Tichborne
with text by Bryan Tichborne

GORDON ELL *The Bush Press* AUCKLAND

DEDICATION

To our sons Benjamin, Hugo and Guy, who fed the chickens, the cat, the cockatoo and the fax, whilst we were away on the research trips.

First published in 1990 by
THE BUSH PRESS OF AUCKLAND
Third printing 1997

© Text copyright, Bryan Tichborne, 1990
© Original watercolours copyright, Nancy Tichborne
© Bush Press Communications Ltd, 1990

Selected from the *New Zealand Trout Fly Calendars*
published by the New Zealand Calendar Company
P.O. Box 1653, Rotorua, New Zealand, 1987-1991

Designed by Gordon Ell, The Bush Press
Typeset by Jacobsons Graphic Communications

Printed in Hong Kong through
Bookprint Consultants Ltd, Wellington, N.Z.

Published by Bush Press Communications Ltd
P.O. Box 33-029, Takapuna, Auckland 9, N.Z.

ISBN 0-908608-50-0

Publisher's Note

As this book was being prepared for the printer, the Government changed the basis of managing fresh-water game fishing in New Zealand, from a series of district and local Acclimatisation Societies to a new group of Fish and Game Councils. The old system had served for well over 100 years. For this reason references to the Acclimatisation Society movement have been retained in the text, as it was originally published, and as it acknowledges the interests and service of many contributors to the original Calendars.

CONTENTS

FAVOURITE FISHING WATERS OF NEW ZEALAND
AND THE FLIES TO FISH THEM WITH
Explored from North to South, on Pages 16 to 111

SOME NOTES ON FISHING IN NEW ZEALAND

HAMILL'S KILLER

FOREWORD

GREENWELL'S GLORY

The New Zealand Calendar Company, the brainchild of Rotorua couple Nancy and Bryan Tichborne, has truly established itself with a string of calendars that since inception in 1985, have annually graced many a kitchen, lounge, study or fishing den.

The first calendar the Tichbornes produced was the New Zealand Trout Fly Calendar. At the time Bryan was advertising manager for a New Zealand fishing-tackle manufacturer and distributor and Nancy had established herself as a book illustrator, and a garden and landscape designer. She had several books to her credit; the most notable was the highly successful *The Cook's Garden* written in conjunction with her two sisters.

Calendars were, however, a totally different field. Calendars date quickly — once the year has started they are in danger of not being saleable. Bryan, with his astute marketing skills, was aware and sensitive to the market. Above all, he could see that a calendar based on top trout-fishing spots around New Zealand, had great potential appeal.

It's now history that the calendars became "best sellers".

The success is entirely due to their combined talents. Take Nancy's sensitive and subtle art style, her eye for the moods and atmosphere of landscapes and particularly trout rivers, join it with Bryan's trout fishing knowledge, his ability to relax people with his warm personality (and in the case of secretive trout anglers, get them to tell of their favourite rivers and flies), and his writing skills to get that information succinctly condensed for calendar form and then add the shared enthusiasm, dedication, imagination and great personalities of the two, and the recipe spells success. The product, in a series of calendars, has become a collectors' item. Add an innovative publishing firm, like Gordon Ell's Bush Press, and you've got *Anglers' Paradise* which will mean, in essence, that the trout-fly calendar work of the Tichbornes is presented in an impressive volume. This should be not only an irresistible attraction to trout anglers, both here and overseas, but, because of Nancy's art work, it should also grace many a coffee table

This volume is one to treasure and marks another step in New Zealand's trout-fishing literature.

TONY ORMAN
Plimmerton, New Zealand

NANCY AND BRYAN TICHBORNE

INTRODUCTION

When publisher Gordon Ell approached us with the idea of this book, we were delighted. The *1991 New Zealand Trout Fly Calendar* is the last in a series of seven calendars featuring my wife Nancy's watercolour paintings and it seemed the perfect time to incorporate a selection from the five landscape-style calendars into a book.

It was a poster Nancy painted for the then New Zealand Forest Service that originally sparked off the idea for these calendars. On this she had featured a giant dragonfly. When I saw this, being a fly fisherman, I thought a selection of trout flies painted in a similar fashion could be a winner. A little earlier a Wellington bookseller friend John Ahradsen had suggested to Nancy that she and her two sisters should capitalise on their successful book *The Cook's Garden* by bringing out a calendar . . . Thus, in this convoluted way, the *New Zealand Trout Fly Calendar* was born.

Nancy and I met in Killarney, Ireland, in the spring of 1961. She was an 18-year-young art student from Dunedin and I was an 18-year-old Sandhurst cadet. She was looking for beautiful places to paint and I realise now that I was looking for beautiful young women looking for places to paint. We got engaged in London, married in Hong Kong and spent the first few years of married life "following the flag" in South East Asia, Europe and Canada. I think we lived in eleven different homes in those years! It was fun but when our first son arrived on the scene in South Wales and I was posted to Aden we decided it was time to "settle down". So I resigned my commission and we set sail, or more correctly, wings, for New Zealand. Soon after we arrived my brother-in-law dragged me off to go fishing in some place called Queenstown. What is more I somehow caught a trout, I suspect not a very bright one, and was myself hooked.

Over the next decade I tried to settle into a corporate existence — by choosing to work for a fishing tackle company I thought this would be the ideal life. However the realities of being a "company man" eventually palled and I was more than ready for my third career when it presented itself. Nancy in the meantime, in between producing three sons, had carved out for herself a successful landscaping business. She loves anything green and this plus her artistic ability made landscape designing a suitable occupation. However she too was ready for a change when it came.

Our first ("1985") trout calendar was a modest affair with Nancy painting between directing bulldozers and me writing text late at night. To our utter amazement and joy it sold out in three weeks. To make sure this was not just a flash in the pan we produced "1986" and even upped the print-run. This too sold out! We now knew we were committed. One memorable evening, during one of our many "think tanks" in a steamy Rotorua hot pool, we decided to make the move. To hell with mortgages, regular salary cheques and gold watches! The boys were ready for a little hardship and independence. So, in common parlance, we went for it.

Since then we have never looked back. We have had our ups and downs — the inevitable compromises involved in four-colour printing, wharf stoppages and customers who mysteriously run out of money just on due date. But the calendars have given us a lifestyle and income that have made it all worthwhile.

As one of our many guides and mentors once said: "You two are indeed fortunate. Here you are visiting all these wonderful lakes and rivers and it is *tax deductible!*" He was right of course — in the course of our travels the length and breadth of New Zealand we have been fortunate enough to have visited literally hundreds of superb fishing spots. Some of these will be forever unpublished (we value our lives) but all of them would have the average overseas angler drooling with excitement. The beauty and solitude of many of our fishing locations is simply staggering — we have become aware of this, plus of course the fragility of it all too . . .

HARE & COPPER NYMPH

People too have made our calendar work enjoyable. Many tiers willingly and expertly contributed flies: people like John Morton (and who could ever forget John) whose creations have featured in all seven calendars; plus Basil Jackson, Garth Coghill, Martin Langlands, Hugh McDowell, Bronwyn Wilson, Steve Willis, Nigel Birt, Norman Marsh, Tony Entwistle and Tony Orman, just to mention a few. The full list of contributors is extensive and is to be found elsewhere in this book. Nancy found it a real challenge to make art out of other people's art which is what fly tying is. The creativity and innovation of New Zealand fly tiers is brilliant. We also have a debt of thanks to all the nice people who assisted in other ways: the many local experts who gave of their time and energy to help us; the kind folk who accommodated and fed us. This list too, is large and is reproduced elsewhere in the book. Indeed without all this incredible, friendly help our calendars would probably not have come to fruition and certainly would never have been so successful.

Looking back over the last five years that we have been publishing the "landscape-style" fishing calendars there have been many occasions worth recalling:

The Lochy River near Queenstown — Roy Moss, ex-Hong Kong cop and now professional fishing guide, taking us to his slice of heaven. Suddenly all interest in fishing stops as Roy has to show us "his" pair of New Zealand native falcons. The air was crisp, the sky blue and everything was right with the world. And this was pre-Gorbachev too.

The Mangles River — Tony Entwistle, another top guide, showing us the fish that Wilbur Smith plus several other household names had caught and released. It was huge and brown, sitting there in dappled sunlight very contentedly, waiting to do its next bit for the New Zealand tourist industry. We were not actually blindfolded going into this particular area but needless to say it is not the one featured.

The Waipa River, King Country — a tranquil stretch of water with native bush on one side and rich dairy land on the other. Appropriately our adviser on this occasion was Graeme Marx who loves his cows as much as his fish.

The legendary Mataura River in Southland — Norman Marsh showing us this river. It has echoes of those famous English chalk streams and Nancy painted a figure who could have easily been taken for Izaak Walton, changing flies, on its banks.

Lake Alexandrina in South Canterbury — Peter Shutt, as enthusiastic as a schoolboy, striding round the edges — delighted to give us and our readers any information he could. Who said anglers were secretive, selfish people! The trees on the skyline that Nancy very nearly left out for reasons of composition . . . Thank goodness she didn't! A great number of anglers have had their ashes scattered under it.

The Tongaririo Delta — anchoring next to another boat to find it was an Auckland friend. It was a weekday and I hope he had his boss's permisssion to be there — mine was in the boat with me taking pictures.

The Tukituki River, Hawkes Bay — young Mark Sherburn concerned that Nancy wanted to paint him with a fish on . . . "The season doesn't open until tomorrow!" For the record the artist used her licence.

The Hutt River, Wellington — Steve Smith, local acclimatisation field officer took us all over this fine river. Where else in the world can one catch well conditioned wild trout so close to a capital city? These trout are safe with people like Steve looking after their interests and anglers are richer for the efforts of a few such enthusiasts.

Lake Brunner, Westland — very few people, lots of trout. A world-class lodge, with accommodation and great meals, plus solitude in copious quantities. Who cares if it rains a little!

CRAIG'S NIGHT-TIME

The Waipahi River, South Otago — the late Bill McLay taking Nancy to see one of his special waterways. We'll miss Bill, he was one of life's gentlemen, a true angler and patient adviser. Otago anglers will miss him too — he did tremendous work for his adopted province.

The Eglinton River, Southland — wading up this crystal clear and icy-cold river with Trevor Halford. Seeing deer sign on the sandy banks, abundant wildlife and Nancy's arm only sticking out of the water with her indispensable camera high and dry but the rest of her most definitely not! The birds learnt some new words that day.

Lake Mapourika, South Westland — getting up at sparrow's chirp to photograph this beautiful lake and having to wait until noon in freezing temperatures for the mist to lift enough to get good shots through it.

The Rangitikei River, central North Island — being in a raft with Yankiwi guide Jack MacKenzie, who can still yell with pure pleasure when he hooks a fish — this after countless prior occasions! Jack's enthusiasm for fishing this river puts the whole of our trout fishing in New Zealand into perspective. We are really very fortunate to have all these wonderful places and wild trout and should never forget that.

The Waiteti Stream Mouth, Lake Rotorua — that irrepressible Scot, John Brown, waxing lyrical about his chosen stream-mouth. We have it on reliable information that he often fishes with one hand on his rod and the other clutching his mobile phone — so he doesn't miss any bookings for his motel.

The Poutu Pool, Tongariro River — wandering up and down the banks of this mighty river. Meeting all manner of folk from John Ross, formerly New Zealand consul-general in New York, to Dr John Kent, author of a new book on fishing the North Island. Who said the Tongariro was an unfriendly place? As Nancy was taking the final shots for this page, a young Maori angler caught and landed a huge rainbow.

The Mangatainoka River — here we experienced real small town hospitality from people like Dianne and Larry Cotter, Keith Fergus and Dawn and Cliff Fergus. Seeing how fishing brings the whole community together for the annual trout carnival was an eye-opener. A lot of fun and a lot of tall stories.

The Upper Wairau River — seeing at first hand what damage could be brought about by "progress". We were happy to be able to campaign in our text against the proposed damming (damning) of this lovely river. A magical day spent with Tony Entwistle.

The Greenstone and Clinton Rivers — a chance to combine calendar research with guided walks through some of New Zealand's more remote and beautiful areas. The Greenstone Valley Walk and Milford Track are tourist gems and we still sigh with nostalgia when we turn up photos of these wonderful, wild and majestic areas. And fish! I have never seen so many fish in a river as we saw in the Clinton. The trouble is all of them bar two saw me too. New Zealand may be going through a recession but have the more affluent nations got anything like the Milford Track?

The Ngaruroro River, Hawkes Bay — scrambling down a sheer precipice carrying very little, with guide Dave Mabin ahead of us like a mountain goat, weighed down with provisions, tackle and an uninflated inflatable boat! Good All Black front-row material that man. The camp Dave had set up reminded me of Kenyan bush camps I had frequented in my youth. But the pre-dinner gin and tonic was an improvement. Dave treats his clients to cordon bleu sophistication in a real wilderness environment.

The Motueka River — having guide Graeme Marshall spend all day showing us this lovely river and repaying him by allowing the typesetting gremlins to adjust the text to ''Graeme Marshall *lies* on the Motueka . . .'' Fortunately Graeme has a sense of humour.

The Pomahaka River — miles away from anywhere with veteran guide Bert Harvey. The artist's husband and pack mule decides to seek even further isolation for a short while . . . Right on cue two Air Force jet fighters go thundering overhead at zero plus 60 feet! We were in a low flying zone. Bert reckons they don't affect the fishing — I can vouch for the fact that they do wonders for other things.

Lake Emily, Ashburton Lakes area — an amazing central Canterbury day spent with Jim Ackerley and Derek Smitheram. We witnessed the dramatic clash of two opposing weather systems and saw Jim's beloved Southern Crested Grebes nesting. Jim's delightful bach at Clearwater was once one-half of the old Ashburton ''picture theatre''. He certainly gave us the dress-circle treatment.

The Manganui-o-teao River — memories of rushing up and down steep bush-covered ravines with Harry Brown. He was at war when we were infants and has synthetic hip joints but it doesn't slow him down. Here too we saw a pair of rare Blue Mountain Ducks at close quarters — yet another tough day at the office!

The Otaki River — spending the day in the good company of Bridget Woodrow and Tony Orman. A splendid trout river so close to population centres but did we see anyone else all day? Not a soul. We'll think of that day when we're next riding the rapid transit system in Hong Kong . . .

Diamond Lake, near Queenstown — being literally in Paradise. The local area is called just that and with every justification. Champagne breakfast on a deserted beach with Anne and Rod Stewart — life can be hell.

The Upper Mohaka River, Kaimanawas — watching guide Ken Duncan, fly fishing, with daughter Katie fast asleep in a carrier on his back. A five hour walk-in and out — through glorious native bush resounding to the calls of the prolific bird life. Acid rain and its dire effects are a whole world away, thank goodness.

The La Fontaine Stream, South Westland — guide Ali Thompson unable to hold himself back when presented with a stream holding fish and no clients to look after! Nancy had no trouble with a model this time even if his motivation was of a different kind. Lynn's kind hospitality ended a perfect day.

The Hakataramea River, South Canterbury — Graeme Warren explaining with great feeling why we all must "Save the Waitaki" and in doing so the "Haka". Nancy's tears on the realisation that this was the sixtieth and final spot on our "watercolour calendar" research trail.

The time had come to move on to something new but we will always remember the people and places connected with those sixty locations. There is something very special about New Zealand's uncrowded and wild fishing places. If Nancy has been able to capture some of this feeling with her watercolours then we have achieved our aim.

HAIRY DOG

In addition to New Zealand our calendars have been sold in North America, Holland and Australia. We have sent individual copies to such unlikely places as Nairobi, Honiara, Saudi Arabia and Jakarta. We know they have been stuck up in offices, dens and loos all over the country. Once Nancy was in Wellington on a bleak wintry evening. Looking up at a big office block opposite her, she suddenly became aware of at least three of her calendars on office walls. Suddenly, Wellington became much warmer.

We are delighted that so many people have enjoyed the calendars and feel very fortunate to have stumbled on such a pleasant and rewarding way to make a living. It gives Nancy great pleasure to think that her artwork is spread so far and wide. I have learnt a lot about marketing and a little about writing. The fact that we now have a publisher in North America exclusively handling all our work is exciting and we enjoy our regular trips to liaise with him in Oregon. Perhaps the aspect I enjoy most about our work is that we have become a good team — sometimes we argue about who makes the tea, but we have become a close-knit business team. Not many husbands and wives get the opportunity to do that.

We will continue with a trout fishing calendar, utilising photographs instead of artwork. Nancy wants to explore new subjects with her watercolours. But we will never forget that it was the *New Zealand Trout Fly Calendar* that gave us the break and changed our lives forever.

BRYAN TICHBORNE
Rotorua, July 1990

TAUPO TIGER

Lake Ototoa, South Kaipara Peninsula

Trout fishing enthusiasts in the Auckland area are normally resigned to spending a great deal of time, money and effort to reach suitable localities. There is, however, very reasonable trout fishing available on their back doorstep so to speak — namely in Lake Ototoa, one of 35 dune lakes situated on the South Kaipara Head near Helensville.

This lake was first stocked with rainbow trout in 1912, apparently unsuccessfully. Further liberations were made in 1928, 1949 and 1953 — with reports of 6 to 8lb trout being caught in that period. In 1982 the Auckland Acclimatisation Society liberated 1,000 rainbow fingerlings — "to provide acceptable trout fishing within reach of the greater Auckland area." There were some problems with the natural food chain and stocking was discontinued to let this strengthen.

Despite this Ototoa has provided reasonable angling in very pleasant surroundings for the past seven years. The average trout tend to be small, around 0.7kg but fish up to 3kg have been taken. The lake also holds rudd and tench as well as a rare population of land-locked banded kokopu (*Galaxia fasciatus*). Koura are plentiful and the dwarf inanga has made a come-back. So the signs are good for the lake to once again become a first-class trout fishery.

Access is by a legal right-of-way running off Donohue's Road — there is a sign and stile over the fence just above the lake. No powered boats are permitted but a dinghy can be carried down from the road. Fly fishing, spinning, trolling and bait fishing are all allowed — with a licence of course. Two thirds of the shoreline is easily accessible to the angler on foot. This is a deep lake (mean depth 12.5 metres) with excellent water quality. It has a small catchment of which half is in exotic forest and native scrub and the remainder is developed farmland, mainly deer farms.

GREEN DOG
Dan Hartley of Mount Wellington is a keen Ototoa angler. This variation of the famous Hairy Dog pattern utilises cream coloured fur from his wife's Tibetan spaniels.

DAN'S COMBINATION
A tandem fly which seems to particularly excite trout when fished deep and retrieved slowly. The "tube fly" with silver body and black and brown squirrel tail, precedes the Red Setter. A Hairy Dog works just as well.

HAMILL'S KILLER
"Killer" pattern lures appear to be most effective in Lake Ototoa. The Hamill's Killer is no exception; it is generally accepted to be an imitation of a bully or dragon fly nymph. Tied here by Basil Jackson; olive-green dyed mallard feathers and red body (which is favoured for night fishing). Has a tail tag of golden pheasant tippet feathers which is now often omitted.

BROWN AND WHITE MARABOU
Marabou flies have become popular in recent years. The pulsating action of the feathers under water is obviously incredibly tempting to trout. This lure is one of an infinitely possible variety but its particular colour combination seems to work well in Ototoa.

PARSONS' GLORY
Often said to resemble a fingerling trout, this is another traditional New Zealand pattern. The yellow body is popular for daylight fishing. Especially deadly in low water conditions but effective in Ototoa any time.

SCOTCH POACHER
An excellent night lure which has its origins in the Rotorua area. Has been found to be useful in Lake Ototoa on overcast days.

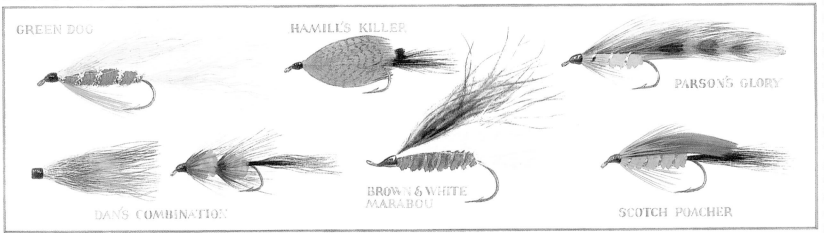

GREEN DOG

HAMILL'S KILLER

PARSON'S GLORY

DAN'S COMBINATION

BROWN & WHITE
MARABOU

SCOTCH POACHER

Waipapa River, Northland

BARRY'S SMELT

NORTHERN RABBIT

SUICIDE NYMPH

MINI-BLACK RABBIT

GREEN NYMPH

PEACOCK NYMPH

PARSONS' GLORY var.

It often astounds the rest of New Zealand that there are actually trout north of Whangarei! In fact there are 15 rivers and lakes containing trout.

The beautiful Waipapa River, which flows through breathtaking native bush scenery into the Hokianga Harbour, is 10 km northwest of Okaihau on State Highway 1. There is easy access from the Forest Road carpark, upstream along the river, via an old bush railway and an 8 km marked trampers' track. The river forks upstream at the Mangapa stream and has its headwaters deep in the Puketi State Kauri Forest. This is a huge watershed rather prone to flooding in winter. However the river clears quickly and has the clearest and coldest trout water in the Bay of Islands Acclimatisation Society district.

Hard-fighting, wild rainbow trout, averaging 0.6 kg and up to 2.1 kg, are to be found the full length of the Waipapa, down to the Rahiri Bridge where it becomes tidal. The good condition of these fish is due to a healthy diet of mayfly, dragonfly and stonefly nymphs, horned caddis, bullies and whitebait/smelt, plus cicadas and manuka beetles in summer.

Fishing is available all year round with the best months being around April and August when the whitebait run up the river. Daily limit bag is 10 trout; minimum size is 25 cm.

Local anglers, like Barry Birchall of Kaikohe, practise and preach catch and release. Barry, an art teacher at Okaihau College, is also a keen fly tier. His favourite Waipapa patterns follow:

BARRY'S SMELT
An excellent summer fly utilising yellow marabou for the tail, a silver lurex yarn body and white or grey rabbit wing tied "bugsbunny" style. Overwing of pearl flashabou.

NORTHERN RABBIT
Barry's top trout fly fishes well in slightly dirty water, at change of light and in bush-shaded areas. He has also used this fly to great effect on the Tongariro.

SUICIDE NYMPH
A variation of the Auckland tier R.W. Berry's nymph pattern. Again very useful in shaded runs. Thorax is a mixture of black synthetic seal's fur or black possum, with some orange synthetic fibre from an old sofa.

MINI-BLACK RABBIT
A lure Barry uses on the Waipapa in winter time and on dark. Hook size 8 to 10. Overwing is a tuft of natural black rabbit fur tied in above the red wool tail and again at the head. Body of black floss.

GREEN NYMPH
Originally this had peacock herl spaced around the khaki wool abdomen to suggest segments but Barry found it worked better for him after this had been chewed off. Also useful in the Kai Iwi Lakes north of Dargaville, when fish are just in the sub-surface layer.

PEACOCK NYMPH
A good general purpose nymph and a variation of the Half Back. Barry lightly weights it with copper or lead wire and fishes it up the runs in summer.

PARSONS' GLORY VARIANT
Used in hook sizes 4 to 8 this is a most successful Waipapa early season fly. Imitating the many smelt and bullies in the river at the time. Orange hackle tail tied below a brown marabou wing, yellow chenille body ribbed with silver oval tinsel. Tinsel also ties down the brown marabou overwing at head. Finished off with an orange hackle.

McLaren Lake, Tauranga District

This scenic lake lies close to Tauranga city, with access off State Highway 29 onto McLaren's Falls Road. It is set in a beautiful park containing an interesting variety of specimen trees — a perfect picnic spot in fact. Fly fishing can be enjoyed there either from the shore or a dinghy. McLaren Lake produces rainbow trout up to 1kg plus and browns to 2kg plus. It is restocked annually, with fish of both species, from the Ngongotaha hatchery. The lake offers these fish a rich and varied diet including mayflies, caddisflies, dragonflies and snails.

Local fishing and hunting guide, Ken Duncan of Tauranga, enjoys his regular fishing trips to the lake and nearby hydro canal. He has established that, in addition to regular evening rises, surface feeding fish are often evident through the day too. This enables Ken to fish the dry fly a lot of the time although he finds nymphs useful. The canal fishes best in the evenings.

When not guiding Ken is resident angling and hunting adviser at Guy and Wright Sports of Tauranga. He is an enthusiastic fly tier — five of his favourites for McLaren Lake follow:

HARE & COPPER
One of the simplest of all nymph patterns to tie and yet one of the most effective. Ken prefers to fish it on a floating line.

PHEASANT TAIL
Another traditional nymph of great importance to the New Zealand angler. In fact this and the Hare & Copper would be the country's most popular nymphs.

GLO NYMPH
A pattern Ken brings out when all else fails! Peacock herl, yellow chenille, ginger hackle and swannundaze wingcase. It seems to be able to trigger a response in selective trout.

BLACK STONE NYMPH
A good general purpose fly which Ken finds takes fish at McLaren Lake. Designed to represent a wide variety of insect life.

KEN'S IRRESISTIBLE
Variant of a famous American dry fly pattern. Ken adds the distinctive white wings to give extra visibility. As with all his flies he uses barbless hooks, thus minimising damage and stress to released fish.

COCH-Y-BONDHU
When various beetles are on the wing in New Zealand this traditional Welsh pattern is unbeatable. Tied here by Basil Jackson of Rotorua, it also represents a large number of other insects that are attractive to trout.

GREEN BEETLE
Again for use when beetles are swarming and dropping onto the water. This fly imitates more closely the manuka beetle (*Pyronata festiva*).

DRAGONFLY NYMPH
An insect often found inside lake trout. The naturals are thought to have a very slow rate of growth and may take up to six years to reach maturity. Pat O'Keefe's pattern here is a remarkable likeness to the real thing. According to Pat the trout think so too!

Waipa River, King Country/Waikato

The Waipa is the largest tributary of the Waikato River. It is also important as the main spawning stream for rainbow trout in the area. There is a mix of rainbows and browns in the Waipa and a wide variety of fishing is available.

The painting is of a spot upstream of Otorohanga and downstream of the Toa Bridge. This locality particularly favours the fly fisherman. The Waipa is an attractive river flowing through both dairy farms and pockets of beautiful native bush. Best fishing is between February-March but fishing can be good all year round — note that some areas of the river have a closed season. Access is relatively easy for much of its length. Stock, gates and fences should be treated with the usual respect.

COCH-Y-BONDHU
The great little trout catcher with the tricky Welsh name. It imitates a large number of terrestrial insects including the green beetle (*Pyronota festiva*). When these beetles are on the water this dry fly can be a devastating fish fooler. Tied here by a keen Waipa angler, Alan Hall of Hamilton.

BROWN BEETLE
This fly imitates the brown or grass grub beetle (*Costelytra zealandica*), a pest much loathed by farmers and loved by trout. Tied by Garth Coghill.

LACE WINGS
Leaf hopper insects (*Scolypopa australis*) flutter about New Zealand streams early in the new year.

Creating personal variations of this distinctive little insect has always entertained fly tiers. The top version was tied by Alan Hall and the lower one by Clark Reid. Both are fish catchers not just samples of the fly tiers' art.

PALMERED FLY
A style of fly made by winding hackles along the length of the hook shank. Alan Hall sometimes uses these dry flies with a nymph tied on a "dropper". They provide a very sensitive indicator (of the trout taking the nymph below) but are quite often taken themselves by the fish.

HARE AND COPPER NYMPH
Another experienced Hamilton fly fisherman, Graeme Webb, swears by this popular pattern for the Waipa, especially late in the season. Here he uses hare's fur mixed with a dark brown fur which he bravely admits borrowing from his mother-in-law's fur coat. Graeme includes a beard hackle on this variation and calls it "Mother-in-law's Wrath".

JACOB'S NYMPH
Another Webb special tied from dyed pheasant tail which is fastened with thin copper wire. The thorax is built up using rabbit fur and again fur from the aforementioned coat — dyed with the pheasant tail.

PEACOCK NYMPH
Alan Hall use this attractive nymph early in the season. Copper wire is wrapped around peacock herl. This relatively simple pattern can bring the angler exciting sport.

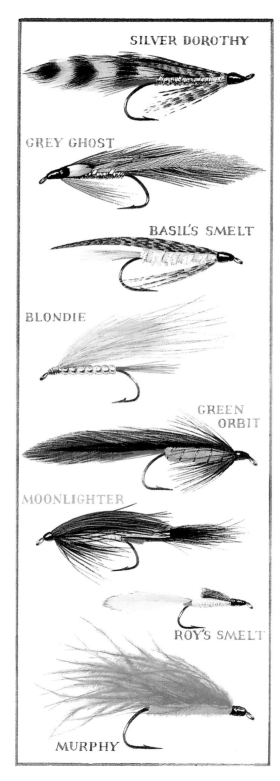

SILVER DOROTHY

GREY GHOST

BASIL'S SMELT

BLONDIE

GREEN ORBIT

MOONLIGHTER

ROY'S SMELT

MURPHY

Lake Rotoiti, Rotorua

Lake Rotoiti is a deep lake (mean depth is 31 metres) which has few spawning streams. It is regularly stocked to ensure anglers have access to a particularly well-conditioned class of fish. In fact Rotoiti now rivals Lake Tarawera for trophy fish, mainly rainbows, with the occasional big brown. Trolling is the most popular method of fishing but there is good fly fishing to be found in many places around the lake.

Hinehopu, at the eastern end, is one of these. There a drainage pipe, which introduces water from a nearby swampy area, obviously attracts trout. "The Pipe" has become an area where good fish are often caught, especially late in the season. Apart from the length of shoreline between Ruato and Hinehopu, which is open 12 months, the rest of the lake has an open season from 1 October to 30 June.

Basil Jackson is a retired school principal and a Rotoiti fishing veteran. Over the years he has worked out which lures work best on Rotoiti. A perfectionist in the art of fly tying, Basil has supplied these three flies:

SILVER DOROTHY
Popular at Rotoiti especially early morning and at dusk. Basil has modified the standard pattern by adding a mallard cap and beard hackle to give more emphasis to the head. An excellent harling lure too.

GREY GHOST
Probably New Zealand's most popular smelt pattern. Wing colour can be varied from very light grey to a sooty shade, to suit conditions. The jungle-cock eye seems to make this lure even more effective.

BASIL'S SMELT
Another good smelt imitation. Artificial polar bear underwing, silver banded body with yellow luminous strip. Tied here on a long shank hook.

Garth Coghill is a regular contributor to our calendars .A meticulous and innovative tier, he is a frequent visitor to Lake Rotoiti, and has provided these three flies:

BLONDIE
The favourite Rotoiti smelting fly of the late George Ferris, a noted New Zealand fishing writer. Garth has covered the tinsel with transparent swannundaze to give depth to the body. Wing is of fine blonde fox fur.

GREEN ORBIT
Another popular lure for this lake. The fluorescent lime green chenille body is effective in deeper water where it reflects even the slightest light rays.

MOONLIGHTER
Rotoiti anglers were amongst the first in the country to use the "aurora" material on their flies. This beauty of a fly from Garth's vice is a prime example of this. The "glow" is recharged with a torch every few casts.

ROY'S SMELT
Roy McKenzie has fished "The Pipe" more times than he can recall. This is a simple but effective "aurora" pattern which ensures that Roy remains one of the more successful fishermen in the area.

MURPHY
This brightly hued lure is a favourite of Cliff Henderson, a local guide. Cliff's clientele, mainly overseas anglers, seldom go home troutless! The dyed orange marabou gives the lure great life under water.

Waiteti Stream Mouth, Lake Rotorua

Lake Rotorua is a large shallow lake with nine fishable stream mouths, all with safe wading. This lake is a truly amazing fishery, despite man's best efforts to ruin it as such. Lake Rotorua is surrounded by either farmland or human habitation and thus has a minimal natural filter to protect water quality. Clarity has diminished over the years and weed flourishes.

In spite of this Lake Rotorua has somehow remained a great trout lake, delighting tourists and locals alike. One of Rotorua's most experienced fishing guides, Bryan Colman, has fished the lake for 46 years and kept meticulous records as a full-time operator for the past 19. These show that Rotorua trout are improving in quality — from an average condition factor of 42 to 54 in fact. His catch rate is up from .97 to 1.41 per hour and the average number of fish caught per angler went from 1.2 to 1.5 . . . the signs of a healthy lake.

All fish, except a few introduced to monitor growth rates, are wild stock. predominantly rainbows averaging 1 to 1.5kg with a few browns which are mainly taken by fly fishermen and can go over 4kg. The lake itself is open all year but the streams close from 1 July to 1 December.

From April onwards large numbers of fish run up the main spawning streams including the Waiteti. A local motelier, John Brown, can often be found fishing the mouth, with cordless phone at the ready for any business calls. He favours standard patterns such as Mrs Simpson, Parsons' Glory, Grey Ghost and Black Prince; in sizes 8 or 6. Other useful flies are:

PARSONS' SUNSET
Another lakeside dweller is Hugh McDowell, well known guide and author. This McDowell variation of the famous Parsons' Glory is his most productive Rotorua pattern.

SKINNY MAC
Works best in the warm summer months when fish crowd the cold, spring-fed stream mouths. Variant of Dave McLellan's Ginger Mick variation, again tied by Hugh.

BALLARD'S BEAUTY
Ray Punter of Rainbow Springs enjoys designing practical flies. This harling pattern has shape, flash and movement. It is named after a former colleague at the Springs, Malcolm Ballard, whose very first trout fishing trip was made memorable by the outstanding success of this fly. Harling on Rotorua is best in early summer.

MIDNIGHT MARABOU
A basic but effective stream-mouth lure from Gary Kemsley. Fished deep and retrieved slowly it works particularly well on bright nights.

FETCH'S FOLLY
Designed by veteran Waiteti angler Tony Fetch. Rechargeable (by torch) luminous body. Should be retrieved slowly.

BLACK PRINCE
Standard pattern said to have originated from the Rotorua district. One used and thoroughly recommended by John Brown.

BLACK BURGLAR
One of a series of internationally-known Burglar patterns from George Gatchell of the Crystal Brook Tackle Shop, Waitahanui, Lake Taupo. A great fly for any stream mouth.

IRISH REBEL
Tied by Pat O'Keefe, proprietor of a specialist Rotorua tackle store. Pat was given this effective pattern by a local fishing identity, Ian Colquohoun.

HELEN'S SMELT
Not to be outdone, Pat's wife Helen ties up this nifty little smelt pattern. It has proved to be a top fish catcher.

BETHLEHEM CAT
Dr John Kent is the author of *North Island Trout Fishing Guide*. He ties this fly using the fur from a dead cat he once found on the road near Bethlehem, Bay of Plenty. It has taken six limit bags for John so far — all at stream mouths.

PARSON'S SUNSET

BALLARD'S BEAUTY

FETCH'S FOLLY

SKINNY MAC

MIDNIGHT MARABOU

BLACK PRINCE

IRISH REBEL

BLACK BURGLAR

HELEN'S SMELT

BETHLEHEM CAT

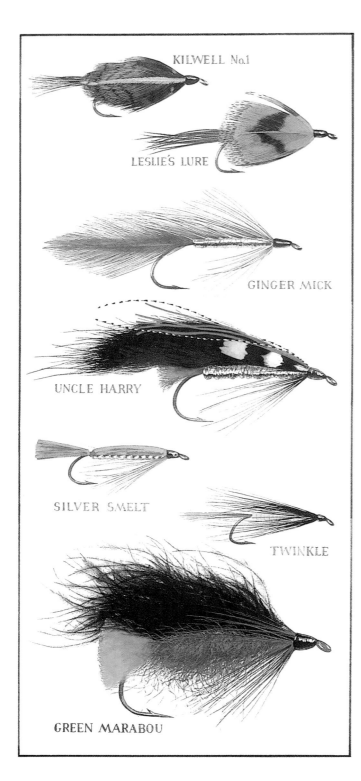

KILWELL No.1

LESLIE'S LURE

GINGER MICK

UNCLE HARRY

SILVER SMELT

TWINKLE

GREEN MARABOU

Te Wairoa Stream Mouth, Lake Tarawera

Round the corner from the Landing is this delightful little stream mouth. Over the years Te Wairoa has produced legendary trout and equally legendary anglers. It holds only five to six rods and fishes best in a good west or south westerly wind. Anglers are advised to stand well back from the lip and cast quickly.

The late Jack Bell was a veteran of many hours fishing this spot. In fact, over the 1960-61 season, Jack caught one percent of the total liberation of three-year-old rainbows — 67 fish in all, averaging an incredible $7^1/_4$ lbs! Whilst he would admit to better results than most, Jack's advice was "lots of hours, lots of practice and lots of luck". We'd add, in his case, it was lots of skill.

Fishing at Te Wairoa for some reasons always starts on 12 April each year. After this date you have to be up very early in the morning to secure a place in the line. It can fish well throughout the legal hours, but be prepared to face disappointing times too.

KILWELL NO.1
Nominated by Jack Bell as the best Te Wairoa fly by far; it must be on a No. 6 hook. Originally developed by Frank Lord, it was at first called the Tarawera Killer and is tied for us here by Hugh McDowell, well-known Rotorua fishing writer and guide. Red body for dull days, yellow for sunny days. Tail is black squirrel tail with sides of brown partridge feathers.

LESLIE'S LURE
Not often seen these days, this pattern used to be popular at Te Wairoa. Created originally by Leslie Newdick, for many years proprietor of the

Spa Hotel, Taupo, it is tied here by Ray Punter of Rainbow Springs, Rotorua. Yellow wool body favoured, tail is cock pheasant tail feather fibres. Body feathers are hen pheasant breast feathers, tied two a side.

GINGER MICK
A close relation of the Parsons' Glory. Again tied by Ray Punter, with a special silver body for Te Wairoa. This variation can be most effective.

UNCLE HARRY
Especially tied by Bronwyn Wilson of Taupo and dedicated to a gentleman who is often seen around Te Wairoa, Harry Tanfield, a popular former Senior Wildlife Officer. Apart from resembling one side of Harry's formidible moustache, it would surely be a great night fly for Te Wairoa!

SILVER SMELT
From Roy Marshall, this neat fly is useful whenever smelt are running. A variation on the "Polystickle" it has raffene for top and tail; clear swannundaze over silver mylar body.

TWINKLE
The past couple of years has seen the use of luminous materials in trout flies. This simple and effective "lumo" fly was tied by Geoff Woodhouse. Regular use of a torch revitalises the luminosity.

GREEN MARABOU
Marabou night flies were developed in New Zealand by Gary Kemsley and have become increasingly popular. This particular one was tied by Nigel Wood of Rotorua, using synthetic seal's fur body, which makes the fly much more durable than chenille. This is just as well, because they get munched a lot.

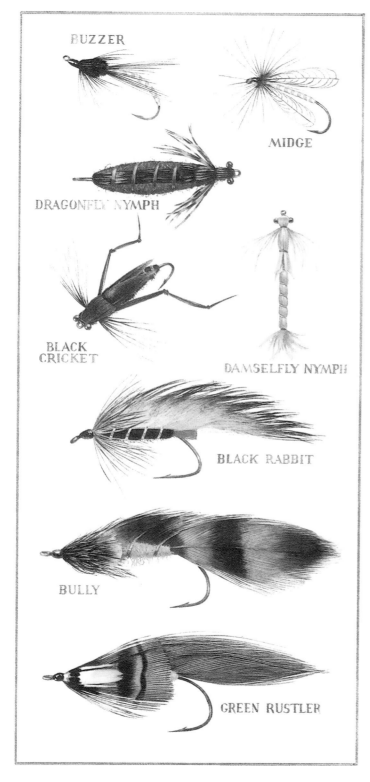

BUZZER

MIDGE

DRAGONFLY NYMPH

BLACK CRICKET

DAMSELFLY NYMPH

BLACK RABBIT

BULLY

GREEN RUSTLER

Lake Aniwhenua, Bay of Plenty

This man-made lake came into being between 1977-1980 when the Aniwhenua Hydro Electric Generating Scheme was implemented on the Rangitaiki River. Lake Aniwhenua covers an area of 255 hectares and has quickly become a rich wildlife resource. Waterfowl including scaup, dabchicks, marsh and swamp crakes, and bitterns are all to be found here. To anglers it is an especially exciting fishery with rainbows and browns often exceeding double figures (lbs.) There are no smelt in this lake but carp, bullies, mosquito fish and the abundant insect life ensures sometimes spectacular growth rates in the trout. It is open all year.

This scene shows the area around the Kopuriki Road bridge — a favourite spot with anglers. The brooding Ureweras form a dramatic back-drop.

Garth Coghill, a well-known Rotorua authority on fly tying, has been an Aniwhenua fan right from the start. He has kindly tied up this interesting miscellany of flies.

BUZZER
The many hatching midge pupae which get caught in the surface film are easy prey for cruising trout. This fly is fished on a long trace and floating line.

MIDGE
It often surprises anglers that the tiny *Chironomidae* nymph is an important food source for trout. This adult ''midge'' should be cast to cruising fish, again on a floating line. Occasional twitches often liven up the proceedings.

DRAGONFLY NYMPH
The *Anisoptera* nymph is a vicious predator which inhabits the lake's margins. Normally slow moving, it is capable of brief turns of speed. Fish this fly deep and try to imitate the natural's movements. Best in early summer.

BLACK CRICKET
Summer is the time many terrestrial insects find their way onto the water and often into trout stomachs. One of the lesser known is the black field cricket *Teleogryllus commodus*. Regarded as a pest by farmers, this Australian import is extremely popular with trout.

DAMSELFLY NYMPH
Zygoptera nymphs (often called ''darning needles'') hatch in summer and ascend to the surface, away from the protection of the weed beds. They are a delicacy for cruising trout. Fish this fly on a floating line, giving the odd twitch to trigger response.

BLACK RABBIT
A great night fly. The soft rabbit fur fibres work and ripple with every movement in the water.

BULLY
The *Gobiomorphus cotidianus* or cockabully is an aggressive and fearless little fish. Too fearless for its own good in fact, for it is a popular item on the trout's menu. Garth's bully imitation must be fished near the bottom with an erratic retrieve.

GREEN RUSTLER
In late autumn and early winter trout gorge themselves on the well established carp population (*Carassius auratus*). When a Mrs Simpson lure fails, Garth finds the Green Rustler most effective.

Lake Rerewhakaiitu, Rotorua District

One of 13 fishable lakes in the district, Rerewhakaiitu covers some 750 hectares and is shallower than most. It is easily accessible from the Rotorua-Murupara highway. It is also unique in that it has a designated "Anglers' Reserve" right round it — helping offset the adverse effects of being encircled by farmland. Limited spawning areas have made it necessary to liberate rainbows, and indeed, over half the fish caught are normally from these liberations.

Open season is 1 October to 30 June with fly fishing being available all round the lake's edges or from an anchored boat. The best fishing is in the cooler months with the Homestead Arm a productive spot. It is an interesting fact that the lake level dropped dramatically during the recent Edgecumbe earthquake. The brooding bulk of Mt. Tarawera adds further interest to an otherwise peaceful pastoral landscape.

Local angler Max Sheffield has fished Rerewhakaiitu for over 30 years. He finds early mornings most productive and maintains that the lake fishes poorly after dark. Trout food sources include koura, dragonfly larvae, smelt and snails.

BLACK MAX
This is a fly Max has evolved especially for the lake. Useful at most times of the day, it really comes into its own during foul weather.

When Maureen and Bill Butler arrived here from Canada 30 years ago, it was Max Sheffield who helped introduce them to Kiwi trout. Both are dedicated Rerewhakaiitu fans and are also committee members of TALTAC — the Turangi-based anglers' organisation. In fact last year Maureen gained the singular honour of being elected the first-ever lady life member of TALTAC. Her flies for Rerewhakaiitu are:

LIMEY
An original MB pattern utilising three shades of thar hair and squirrel tail.

KEELER
Named for another lady, the famous Christine, this showy lure is extremely attractive to the lake's rainbows.

WOOLLY WORM
Maureen's variation of the popular American pattern, palmered right up to the eye.

SIMPLE SALMON
A basic version of a classic salmon fly in everyday dress.

PAT'S DAMSEL
A fly with which Pat O'Keefe of Rotorua has had great success. In size 12 with goose biot tail and deer hair legs.

GOLDEN DEMON
Used by Pat as his "last resort" fly. Gold mylar body.

PAT'S SMELT
Pat Swift, also of Rotorua, came up with this dinky little pattern which incorporates the synthetic material from a big game lure. Perfect when Rerewhakaiitu trout are smelting.

HUGHIE'S MALLARD
Based on a range of old Irish patterns and from the gifted Rotorua fly tier Hugh McDowell, who himself is based on an old Irish pattern. Hughie's book *New Zealand Fly Tying* is a must for anyone interested in the art.

Rangitaiki River, Bay of Plenty

The Rangitaiki rises on Lochinvar Station south of the Taupo-Napier road. It flows through the exotic pines of the huge Kaingaroa Forest, down through Murupara, Lake Aniwhenua and Edgecumbe, to enter the sea near Thornton in the Bay of Plenty. It is an extensive and varied waterway some 155km in length and one of the more important fishing rivers of the North Island.

The Rangitaiki's uppermost waters cut through the pumice lands of the central North Island's volcanic plateau. Down to and including the man-made Lake Aniwhenua there is excellent fly fishing for both brown and rainbow trout up to 4kg. Best fishing is mid-summer but winter fishing (as depicted above) is productive too. The many tributaries of the Rangitaiki also offer great fishing, as does the Whirinaki River which joins it near Murupara.

The area featured above is in these upper reaches. Here one can follow the Rangitaiki for great distances along good forestry roads. Even in the height of summer uncrowded fishable water is easy to find. It is a peaceful, almost wilderness, area.

Most of the river is open to all-year angling but above its confluence with the Otamatea Stream the season opens 1 October and closes 30 June. A Rotorua licence is required as is a permit to enter the Kaingaroa Forest area available free from NZ Timberlands offices in Rotorua and Kaingaroa. When getting this make sure you purchase a map of the forestry roads too. A wide variety of flies are successful on the Rangitaiki:

FREE SWIMMING CADDIS NYMPH
Garth Coghill, a regular visitor to the Rangitaiki, has observed an abundance of the green free-living caddis *Hydrobiosis parumbripennis*. His three flies here represent the insect's life cycle. The nymph is a very active, carnivorous creature which itself is preyed upon by the trout.

PUPA
When free of its cocoon the mature pupa swims about in the water for several hours before rising to become a winged fly. Again it is readily available to predatory fish.

ADULT
Once emerged adult caddisflies don't waste any time. They mate on shore whereupon the females return to the water to lay their eggs. Yet again the trout are on hand to devour the tasty offerings.

WEE GREEN
This is an original pattern from Pat O'Keefe, proprietor of a popular Rotorua fishing tackle shop. Tied on a size 10 hook Pat calls this "a fly for all seasons"

SHOT IN THE DARK
Pat's wife Helen tied up this American-originated pattern. Similarly useful in Rotorua and Taupo rivers.

DANCING CADDIS
Pat Swift works at the O'Keefe store and is also a talented fly tier. This Gary LaFontaine (U.S.) pattern, skated across the surface during a caddis hatch, will tempt even the most selective of Rangitaiki trout. Tied on a size 12, Swedish dry-fly hook.

MURRAY'S MAGIC
A successful nymph pattern regularly used by local fishing guide Murray Downie of Murupara. Tied by David Syme. In sizes 10 or 12, but must be weighted.

MALLARD & CLARET
A "wee wet" from Hugh McDowell author of *New Zealand Fly Tying* and a well known Rotorua fishing guide. A traditional pattern which Hugh finds works well for him on the Rangitaiki.

HUGHIE'S BUG
A fly Hugh first tied whilst living in California. Designed to represent "anything creepie crawlie". Like a large number of American-originated patterns it is extremely successful in New Zealand.

nymph — WEE GREEN — MURRAY'S MAGIC — FREE SWIMMING CADDIS — DANCING CADDIS — HUGHIE'S BUG — adult — pupa — SHOT IN THE DARK — MALLARD & CLARET

BLACK NYMPH

HUGHIE'S BUG

AMBER SWANNUNDAZE

PLUNDERPUSS

BLOW FLY

GREEN BEETLE

GARRETT HATCH

JIMMY SQUIRRELL

Ruakituri River, East Coast

This is one of the great, untamed wilderness rivers of New Zealand. Its origins lie deep in the heart of the rugged Urewera National Park. From there it tumbles, rushes, slows and finally meanders through bushy mountain valleys, gorges and wide river flats, towards the North Island's north-east coast. This is a true back-country river.

The Ruakituri produces some of the largest wild rainbow trout to be encountered in New Zealand, continually yielding these splendid fish to the nymph and dry fly angler. It is an indication of the type of angler fishing these waters that catch and release is a voluntarily accepted norm. This, plus the remote and difficult access, has so far safeguarded what could easily become a threatened fishery.

A regular visitor to the river, both as a professional guide but often just for sheer pleasure, is Hugh McDowell, author of the best-seller *New Zealand Fly Tying*. Hugh has selected three flies he finds useful for the Ruakituri:

BLACK NYMPH
A basic pattern which Hugh says works better in smaller sizes such as 14. He once had a particularly good day using one with a wing-case of green Lurex, so he now always incorporates this.

HUGHIE'S BUG
Developed by Hughie when he lived in Northern California, where he tied flies for the local tackle shop. It has, like its originator, made a happy transition to the Antipodes. Hugh has in fact varied the original a little by substituting oval gold tinsel for the copper wire ribbing and a slip of turkey tail-feather for the latex rubber strip wing-case.

AMBER SWANNUNDAZE
The original pattern and a very hard one to tie nicely. As Hugh points out, the trout fortunately will often forgive an untidy tier, so don't overlook this pattern. In Hugh's experience, this fly takes more browns than rainbows, due perhaps to its light weight and slow sink rate.

Another fly-fishing guide who regularly chooses to drive or fly his clients into the Ruakituri is Ali Thompson. He accommodates them in a cosy riverside bunkhouse on Tuahu Station, deep in the Ruakituri Valley. Having guided on this almost legendary river for many years Ali's recommended patterns are:

PLUNDERPUSS
A very successful dry tied from raccoon and bear's hair. Fished late in the evening, this fly represents some of the large bush moths which tumble onto the water from the overhanging ferns and trees at that time of day.

GREEN BEETLE
Spring and early summer see the emergence of the green beetle in this region of New Zealand and once these tasty morsels begin dropping onto the water, feeding frenzies are often witnessed. The trout position themselves below and downstream of the overhanging canopy.

BLOWFLY
To most, the common blowfly is little more than a buzzing pest. However this little beauty, when used as a dry on the Ruakituri, especially during humid and warm summer days, will give the angler quite a different "buzz". It needs to be presented to slowly cruising trout with the utmost care and skill.

GARRETT HATCH
Spring and early summer are the favoured times to float this little gem of a fly over known lies on the Ruakituri River. Especially where the more narrow, swifter moving waters form a channel between large boulders and then fan out into a slower moving pace.

JIMMY SQUIRRELL
Named like the one above after an American client, this fly also induces savage takes by large trout. When worked upstream, down through fast moving waters and into the depths of the larger pools, this nymph can evoke startling results.

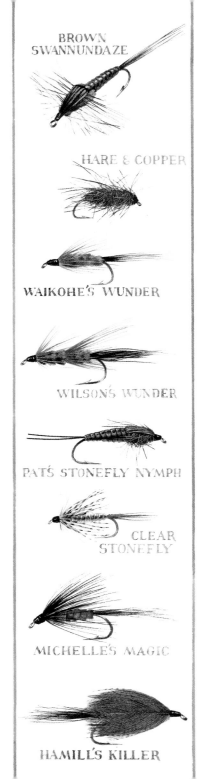

BROWN
SWANNUNDAZE

HARE & COPPER

WAIKOHE'S WUNDER

WILSON'S WUNDER

PAT'S STONEFLY NYMPH

CLEAR
STONEFLY

MICHELLE'S MAGIC

HAMILL'S KILLER

Waiau River, East Coast

This splendid trout river drains the rugged area south of Lake Waikaremoana and flows south-east through farming areas to join the Waikare-Taheke River near Patunamu Forest. From here it runs into the Wairoa River and down to the sea near the township of Wairoa itself.

The best fishing is in the upper reaches from the Putere area up. There are many pools and runs containing mainly rainbows, with some of these up to 3 kg. Season is from 1 October through to 30 June with either a Rotorua or New Zealand tourist licence required.

Brian and Janice Batson of 'Waikohe' are hill country farmers who have diversified into a successful trout-guiding and farm-stay business. They provide access and skilled guiding to some of the best and most difficult-to-get-to bits of the river plus the comforts and hospitality of a typical New Zealand back country farm. The repeat business they get is an indication of their friendly service.

BROWN SWANNUNDAZE
A nymph Brian ties and uses right through the season. On a "dropper" it is especially effective on the Waiau.

HARE & COPPER
If an angler was limited to just one fly Brian says he would use this one! Deadly in all rivers and streams in the area — Brian ties them on a size 12 or 14 hook.

WAIKOHE WUNDER
Excellent when fished as a wet fly on a size 12 hook; especially from November to mid-December when the manuka beetle hatch is on.

WILSON'S WUNDER
Originally tied by Eric Wilson of Turangi for the mighty Tongariro River. Equally good for the Waiau when fished across and down on a sinking line. The white tip on the tail seems to be a great attractor.

PAT'S STONEFLY NYMPH
A good all-round fly from Pat Swift of Rotorua; Monocord tail, Larva Lace body and hare's fur thorax.

CLEAR STONEFLY
Pat O'Keefe, popular proprietor of a specialist tackle store in Rotorua, recommends this fly for the Waiau. Pat uses a green copper underlay, flat clear mono and a partridge hackle overlay.

MICHELLE'S MAGIC
A former tying pupil of Pat O'Keefe's is Michelle Batson — Janice and Brian's 18-year-old daughter. She came up with this little beauty for the area.

HAMILL'S KILLER
A dragonfly nymph imitation which Michelle ties up for the local lakes as well as the river. The Hamill's is a traditional New Zealand pattern which must have accounted for many thousands of trout in its time. Recently it was encountered catching large salmon in Alaska!

Waitahanui River, Lake Taupo

This famous Taupo river rises in the Kaingaroa Forest and flows 25km northwest to enter Lake Taupo at the small lakeside settlement of Waitahanui. It is probably best known for the "Picket Fence" of anglers competing elbow-to-elbow, to catch one of the many trophy fish which attempt to enter the river.

The main scene above is of the Limit Pool, formerly known as the Charlie Brown Pool. This is several kilometres up the river and it is a wily or lucky trout that make it up there when the fishing is on! It will have evaded capture by literally hundreds of keen anglers in the Picket Fence or highway bridge areas. Upstream of the main highway the river has a quite different aspect — meandering and beautiful.

Ann and George Gatchell run the Crystal Brook Tackle Shop immediately north of the Waitahanui river mouth. George is widely known for his unique Burglar patterns and for his skill in landing large Waitahanui trout. A newcomer to the river would be well advised to seek George's advice before fishing it.

Many Crystal Brook flies are from the Wellington commercial tier Allan Rush. George's selection for the area featured is:

HARE & COPPER
An ubiquitous nymph which is to be found in every self-respecting Kiwi angler's fly box.

HALFBACK
Another "must" for the Waitahanui. This nymph comes in many variations and is often thought to be a New Zealand pattern — probably due to its rugby-like title. However, its origins are North American.

BUG EYE
A popular Taupo nymph, originated by Bob

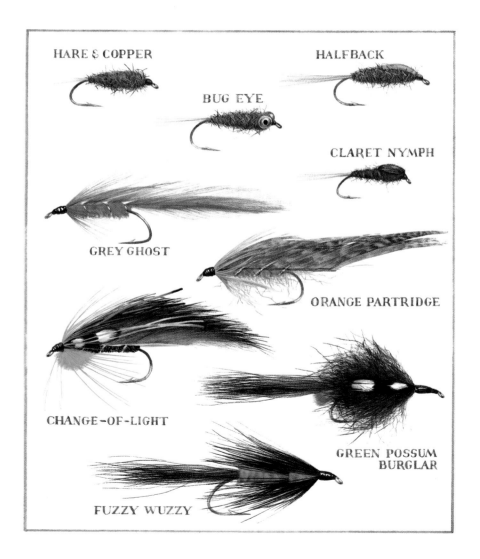

HARE & COPPER

HALFBACK

BUG EYE

CLARET NYMPH

GREY GHOST

ORANGE PARTRIDGE

CHANGE-OF-LIGHT

GREEN POSSUM BURGLAR

FUZZY WUZZY

Christie of the Bridge Lodge, Turangi. Also used extensively on the mighty Tongariro River.

CLARET NYMPH
Another fly George Gatchell says will work well in the Waitahanui.

GREY GHOST
George's daughter-in-law Daphne also ties flies for the shop. This traditional New Zealand smelt fly, in the smaller hook sizes, is as good in the river as at the mouth.

ORANGE PARTRIDGE
Yet another supplier of quality flies to Crystal Brook is Bronwyn Wilson, an accomplished Taupo angler and fly tier. This pattern is a good example of her practical yet handsome work.

CHANGE-OF-LIGHT
Bronwyn's unusual lure is good for just that: those magical fishing interludes at dusk and dawn.

GREEN POSSUM BURGLAR
George's famous Burglars, at least one of which has graced our calendars each year, are much sought after by Waitahanui anglers. The opossum fur used here gives the lure a most lifelike action under water.

FUZZY WUZZY
The fly painted here is an historical one! It is from one of the late "Budge" Hintz's fly boxes. This well-known angler-author retired to live at Taupo after a distinguished career in journalism culminating in his long-term editorship of *The New Zealand Herald*. The Waitahanui was his piscatorial Shangri-La and he fished it every minute he could. This fly, brainchild of the late Fred Fletcher who built and ran the Waitahanui Lodge, is often incorrectly referred to by many anglers as the Hairy Dog. It would be fascinating to know how many Waitahanui trout "Budge" Hintz took on this particular fly.

PUNCH'S PRIDE

PINK PANTHER var.

GREEN ORBIT

YELLOW LADY

DOLL FLY

BARRED BULLY

BUGGLES

Whanganui Bay, Lake Taupo

The Western Bays of Lake Taupo offer both the fly caster and "boatie" great and sometimes spectacular fishing. Whanganui Bay is the smallest and most southerly of these bays.

Punch Wilson's distinctive charter boat *K2* is a regular visitor to Whanganui. It is one of his favourite harling spots. This method of fishing (trolling a fly on a light tackle) enables one to experience the thrill of catching a big Taupo trout on a fly, without leaving the comfort of an all-weather boat. Punch has fished Taupo most of his life and his local knowledge and good humour brings clients back time and time again.

Harling flies are designed to imitate the bait fish which form such an important part of a Taupo trout's diet. Punch's son Gerald ties flies for *K2* use — two of these follow:

PUNCH'S PRIDE
Also known as the Ghostly Lady — a hybridisation of the famous Grey Ghost and Yellow Lady (another fly featured on this page). There are three species of native fish in Lake Taupo, the Koaro *(Galaxias brevipinnis)* the common bully *(Gobiomorphus cotidianus)* and the common smelt *(Retropinna retropinna)*. Smelt were introduced into Lake Taupo between 1934 and 1940, to correct a gradual deterioration in the size of trout apparent at that time. This was a far-sighted move which obviously worked, as many of the flies used today on Lake Taupo are designed to imitate this valuable little fish.

PINK PANTHER VARIANT
Another very effective harling pattern; again tied as a smelt representation. Gerald ties all his harling patterns with four main tail feathers while most commercial ties have only two.

GREEN ORBIT
A favourite with Brian Hussey, another well known Taupo fishing guide and fly tier. Attributed to

Wilfred Beaumont-Orr, an early Taupo tackle dealer, the name is a play on his surname. It was an immediate success in 1930 and remains in common use today.

YELLOW LADY
First introduced to Taupo by Brad Bocket. It was originally a South Island pattern called a Yellow Devil. Bocket added a red head and a wisp of red at the tail. As a launch owner on Taupo for many years he knew a good fly when he harled one. Still a consistent tempter of trout and highly thought of by most of the present commercial boat operators on Lake Taupo.

DOLL FLY
An American pattern which can be used as a harling lure. It is however more often cast to smelting fish by fly fishermen. Recommended especially for the Whanganui in size 6 by Gary Kemsley in his book *Taupo Fishing Guide*. Tier: Tony Hayes of Tongariro Lodge.

BARRED BULLY
This splendid fly is the creative work of Christchurch tier Martin Langlands. The distinctive barring effect is given by the use of four sets of hen pheasant side feathers on each side of the fly. Tied on a long shank, with a dubbed Antron body. Not designed specifically as a harling pattern but what self-respecting trout could refuse an offer like this? Adult male bullies, which spawn in Taupo between August and January, develop dark brown or black breeding colours at this time. They become quite aggressive which makes them even more available to predatory trout.

BUGGLES
A rather "hi-tech" bully imitation with large eyes like the natural. Traditionalists might shy away from this pattern but Martin reports that it does catch fish. Perhaps trout, like humans, enjoy the prospect of the occasional nouveau cuisine.

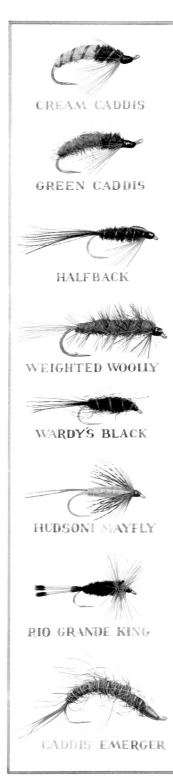

CREAM CADDIS

GREEN CADDIS

HALFBACK

WEIGHTED WOOLLY

WARDY'S BLACK

HUDSONI MAYFLY

RIO GRANDE KING

CADDIS EMERGER

Upper Mohaka River, Kaimanawa Ranges

A true wilderness river in its upper reaches, the Mohaka is formed by the joining of the Oamaru and Kaipo rivers. This is just upstream of the pool illustrated. The Mohaka then runs for 100km, dropping steeply through bushclad gorges, to its mouth in Hawke's Bay.

These upper reaches are for the adventurous or airlifted angler only; access is either by light aircraft or hours of hard tramping. It is a superb area scenically and offers good but not easy fly fishing. Ken Duncan, a Tauranga-based fishing and hunting guide, often brings clients in to stay at the comfortable private hut which is located alongside the airstrip near this spot. Air Charter Taupo operate both helicopters and fixed wing into the area, making access, accommodation and provisioning very easy.

Ken has noticed an increase in the river's rainbow population recently but brown trout still predominate. He recommends a carefully presented nymph with a long, light leader. When hatches occur they can last all day. A long, warm summer's day fishing this river, with Ken as an attentive and skilled guide, is an experience not to be missed. The season runs from 1 October through to 30 June, with the early part giving the best results.

Like most good guides, Ken ties his own flies — four of his suggestions for the upper Mohaka follow:

CREAM CADDIS
At times there can be an abundance of the horny cased caddis in the river. Ken ties up this pattern as a real trout tempter.

GREEN CADDIS
Another Antron-bodied nymph which works well when naturals, *Pycnocentrodes* spp., are around.

HALFBACK
Ken's own personal favourite pattern for the area. With this and Hare & Copper he feels he would not go hungry in a survival situation.

WEIGHTED WOOLLY
A Keith Draper pattern that Ken uses in deep pools or "when all else fails".

WARDY'S BLACK
Dennis Ward of Rotorua, a fellow guide, is another Mohaka fan. This fly of his represents the common stonefly nymph *Zealandaperla* spp., so often found in the river.

HUDSONI MAYFLY
Dennis ties this to imitate an uncommon but significant food source for headwater trout — *Ichthybotus hudsoni*. This is New Zealand's only genus of burrowing mayfly, which can be found in isolated areas such as this. Dennis feels its size attracts large trout.

RIO GRANDE KING
An import used with great success on the Mohaka by one of Dennis's clients, American angler Dan Chapin. Needless to say it is now firmly established in the Ward fly box.

CADDIS EMERGER
Another pattern which has proved its worth in the Mohaka. From Lindsay Lyons, another well-known Rotorua fishing guide.

Tongariro River Delta, Lake Taupo

The mighty Tongariro is one of the world's great trout rivers. It enters Lake Taupo at the "Delta", which consists of four different mouths. Each mouth faces in a different direction, allowing anglers to fly fish in almost any wind. At each mouth the river has formed a shallow shelf which runs out into the lake and then drops off into very deep water.

The most effective method of fishing the Delta is to anchor a boat on the "drop-off". Fly fishing only is permitted — long casts with fast sinking lines, letting them sink very deep and then retrieving slowly.

Good fly fishing is available here all year round. This area produces the biggest numbers of large rainbows in New Zealand. Prolific food sources in the shape of koura and smelt account for this.

It is a tranquil spot on a nice day, with a pleasant view of the cratered Mount Pihanga in the background.

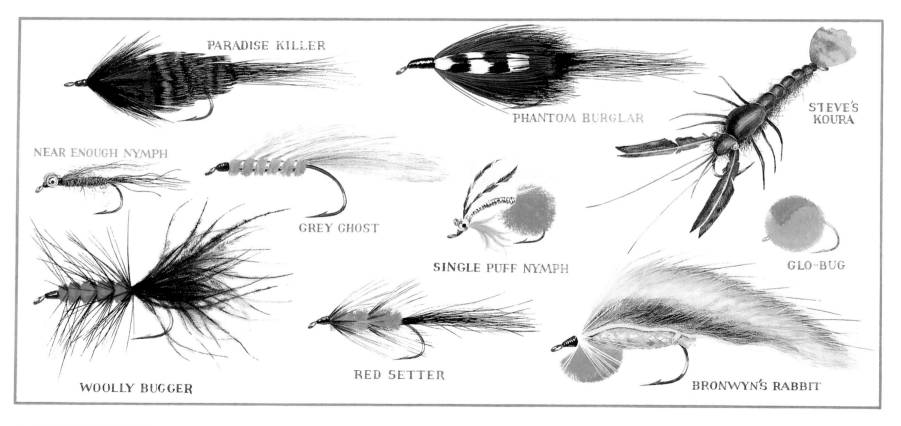

PARADISE KILLER

PHANTOM BURGLAR

STEVE'S KOURA

NEAR ENOUGH NYMPH

GREY GHOST

SINGLE PUFF NYMPH

GLO-BUG

WOOLLY BUGGER

RED SETTER

BRONWYN'S RABBIT

PARADISE KILLER

Tied in the New Zealand "Killer" pattern style but with Paradise Duck belly feathers. The rabbit fur collar gives the lure a real "bully" head effect. Imaginatively tied by Herb Spannagl, an Austrian-Kiwi angler.

PHANTOM BURGLAR

George Gatchell of the Crystal Brook Tackle Shop, Waitahanui, is the originator of these distinctive and deadly lures. Drop in and have a chat to George some time and admire his Burglars!

STEVE'S KOURA

Steven Willis of Christchurch tied this immaculate representation of one of the trout's favourite delicacies. He advises that it is strictly speaking a copy of the South Island freshwater crayfish. We don't think Delta trout would be parochial Steve! It is interesting to note that, until recently, koura imitations were banned.

NEAR ENOUGH NYMPH

The "bathtub eyes" have it! A most successful nymph from David Dannefaerd of Sutherlands Sports, New Plymouth.

GREY GHOST

Tony Hayes of Tongariro Lodge swears by this popular smelt imitation. Like most good flies it is a simple pattern. The fluorescent green chenille body seems especially good at the Delta.

SINGLE PUFF NYMPH

From the artistic vice of Bronwyn Wilson of Taupo. Devastatingly attractive to trout.

GLO-BUG

The cause of considerable apoplexy when first introduced to New Zealanders, the Glo-Bug has now been accepted by most anglers.

WOOLLY BUGGER

An American pattern which has proved an excellent koura imitation at the Delta.

RED SETTER

Probably the most consistent lure there is for taking lake-run trout. The creation of former Turangi identity Geoff Sanderson.

BRONWYN'S RABBIT

Another beautiful Wilson creation. Rabbit strip, flashabou tubing and orange puff combine to form a highly successful lure.

LEMON WICKHAM'S

GREEN FLASHBACK

GREY NYMPH

BOB'S BUGEYE

HARWOOD'S CLARET

GALAH

RED RABBIT

LESLIE'S LURE

Poutu Pool, Tongariro River, Turangi

Thousands of anglers are drawn to this river annually, such is its international reputation for large, hard-fighting trout. The Tongariro is not an easy river to fish which is possibly one of its main attractions. With prime fishing between May and September, the angler is often confronted with extreme weather conditons — the "misery factor" can reach very high levels. Wading must be undertaken with care and common sense. It is an intensely satisfying river to fish, however; kilometres of wonderful stretches with numerous pools. It is little wonder that the late Admiral Hickling (of *Freshwater Admiral* fame) chose to spend the rest of his days on the Tongariro. There is a magical quality about this river which captivates anglers from all walks of life.

This river is usually fished either downstream with a wet or upstream using a nymph. The fly must be presented to pass close by the trout who of course has other things on his or her mind. In the main distance casting and fast sinking lines are called for to cover the lies. Flies used are many and varied with perhaps the most famous being the Red Setter. Here are some other patterns used with success on the Tongariro:

LEMON WICKHAM'S
From the innovative and practical vice of Keith Collins, Wellington. Keith, a former winner of the prestigious Veniard's (U.K.) "Swannundaze" Competition finds this fly highly successful in summer when the fishing is normally slow.

GREEN FLASHBACK
In autumn and winter Keith always starts fishing with this pattern. He says it rarely lets him down. Again he has improved on an existing fly, with great results. Do not make the silver mylar "wingcase" too big though.

GREY NYMPH
Tony Hayes is a part-owner and guide at Tongariro Lodge, an internationally acclaimed establishment on the banks of the river. His favourite is this heavily weighted little nymph, a consistently effective fish tempter.

BOB'S BUGEYE
Another well known fishing hostelry is the Bridge Fishing Lodge. Owner-manager Bob Christie originally tied this simple but heavy nymph for his fishing schools. It is now recognised as a leading pattern for the river.

HARWOOD'S CLARET
Frank Harwood is another skilled guide on the Tongariro. Like Admiral Hickling, he is an Englishman who has discovered his angling Utopia. This original pattern is one of four nymphs Frank uses to get outstanding results.

GALAH
John Morton, Christchurch landscape architect, fly tier and regular pilgrim to the Tongariro, always comes up with something a little different. This nymph (originated by Adrian and Malcolm Bell) works as efficiently on the river as it does down south.

One of the Tongariro's better-known anglers is Bob Jones, the property magnate. He finds standard patterns work perfectly well for him:

RED RABBIT
One of the many variations of a great New Zealand lure. Bob switches to this fly when the river is flooding.

LESLIE'S LURE
Originally the creation of Leslie Newdick, for many years the proprietor of the Spa Hotel, Taupo. Bob Jones took a 13lb (5.9kg) rainbow out of the river using a small Leslie's.

Stony River, Taranaki

NEAR ENOUGH NYMPHS

BLACK SPIDER

COCH-Y-BONDHU

HARE & COPPER

LACEWING

SEDGE

RED SETTER PUP

The trout waters of Taranaki radiate from Mt Egmont like the spokes of a bicycle wheel. Their passage to the sea is both short and steep, producing boulder strewn streams with tumbling rapids in between short pools. Although not recognised as providing New Zealand's best fly fishing, these rumbustious waters do provide challenging and rewarding angling.

The Stony is such a river — one of great natural beauty and pristine water quality. Beyond doubt it is the pick of Taranaki's trout streams. Access is easy provided the angler is a confident wader. Rainbow trout predominate in this river although magnificent browns are abundant in the lower reaches. All methods catch fish; however the browns are most frequently taken on the dry fly in the late evening. Opens 1 October, closes 30 April.

It is interesting to record that the Stony was the first river in the North Island with a "Local Conservation Order" placed on it — signifying the unique qualities of this magnificent and historic river.

David Dannefaerd is a local sports-store proprietor and keen angler. Anyone wishing to fish the area would do well to have a chat with David at Sutherlands Sports. David's own ties for this river follow:

NEAR ENOUGH NYMPHS
These two flies are tied with a rough wool body and deer-hair tail. As David says, these nymphs are not out of the ordinary but they are "near enough" to fool Stony fish!

Noel Baty is a popular fishing writer, keen trout angler, New Plymouth resident and a practical fly tier. Although a "Taupo man" by inclination he still enjoys the challenge of Taranaki waters. Noel tied up these flies for the Stony:

BLACK SPIDER
A traditional British fly which has stood the test of time and travel. The glossy black hackle gives the pattern realism and buoyancy.

COCH-Y-BONDHU
The beauty of this other traditional dry fly is that it represents a good many insects right through the season. A Welsh beetle which is recognised by Kiwi trout!

HARE AND COPPER
Yet another standard. This time a deadly effective nymph which works well in the Stony. Underlay of fine copper wire, tail clump of hare fur, body of roughly dubbed hare fur and ostrich herl collar.

SEDGE
Noel's imitation of a local natural. Ostrich herl body, furnace hackle, tail of hackle fibres, wings formed by lacquering pheasant body feather and using a flame and template to get the required shape.

LACE WING
Another Baty special; imitates the leaf hopper insect which abounds in Taranaki. Despite its size trout go to great lengths to devour this insect — and hopefully the fly . . .

RED SETTER PUP
A versatile fly. As the name suggests this fly is "half a Red Setter". Successful in faster water, cast across and allowed to swing, retrieved up along the bank side, or up and around rocks, where a trout may lie.

Manganui-o-teao River, Central North Island

It would be hard to find a more beautiful trout river than this. The Manganui-o-teao rises on the western slopes of Mt Ruapehu and flows through native forest and farm land to its confluence with the Wanganui River. The river is easily accessible to the public for some 30 to 40 km. It is a big, wild and scenic river providing perfect habitat for wildlife, in particular the Blue Mountain Duck, one of only four species of "torrent duck" in the world.

However it is also a vulnerable river. The 1969 and 1975 Ruapehu eruptions caused havoc to the wildlife on and in the river. Thankfully man has at last recognised the value and fragility of this fine river. A National Water Conservation Order was placed on it in 1987. The area depicted above is the Atirohia Reserve, a Queen Elizabeth II National Trust Protected Open Space.

The Manganui-o-teao contains an equal mix of rainbow and brown trout, averaging around 1.5kg. With the heavy flow and deep pools alongside papa cliffs, safe wading is important. Nymphing and the dry fly are recommended methods — mayflies, stoneflies and caddis are prolific. Best months are January through to March.

Harry Brown is a local farmer and Conservancy Council member. He has fished the river for several decades. It is through the efforts of people like Harry that the Conservation Order came about. He recommends the following flies:

BROWN'S STONEFLY
Tied to simulate *Aucklandobius* spp, commonly found in the area. Harry weights this fly and varies the body colour to suit conditions.

HAIRY NYMPH

Harry thinks this probably represents the *Coloburiscus humeralis* mayfly. His wife's llama-hair coat provided such a valuable source of material for this fly that she ended up giving it to him!

SMOOTH CASE CADDIS

An innovative copy of *Olinga feredayi*. Here Harry uses copper wire bound with cassette tape and finished with clear nail varnish.

BRIGHT'S BROWN

Another local angler Chris Bright prefers to fish the evening rise on this river and finds this dry fly very successful.

SHADOW MAYFLY

Visiting English eye surgeon, Richard le Mesurier, swears by this European pattern. He has used it successfully in Yugoslavia, southern England and New Zealand — both on rainbows and browns.

RUAROBBER

Professional guide Ali Thompson finds this attractive dry most effective, especially during the height of summer.

GREEN HALFBACK

Lee Tan is a keen Wellington fly fisher who often visits the Manganui-o-teao. He uses this nymph in slower water and for the tails of pools.

PEACOCK HALFBACK

Lee finds this pattern works well in the faster water and at the heads of pools. A good fly for a river where caddis larvae are so abundant.

HALFBACK RABBIT

OMAHAKI NYMPH

RABBITS

HALFBACK MAGGOT

MABIN'S DRY

NGARURORO SPIDER

Ngaruroro River, Hawkes Bay

This magnificent central Hawkes Bay river with over 50km of fishable water drains a large catchment area, entering the sea just north of Hastings. The Ngaruroro is justifiably famous for the size and superb condition of its rainbow trout. The Ngaruroro's middle reaches offer the adventurous angler some exciting fishing.

Dave Mabin is a local fishing and hunting guide. He takes groups of up to four people (maximum four days) into the Ngaruroro where they stay in a Kenyan-style safari camp in remote bush-covered country. Access is by 4-wheel drive to the edge of the gorge and then by foot down what at first appears to be an impossible 300m high precipice but turns out to be a relatively easy walk in. Helicopter access is available should this be preferred.

Dave's camp is set close-by the river in a delightful kanuka grove. Deer and wild Merino sheep abound in the area. The camp itself is a veritable oasis of comfort — Dave's skill as a host and chef is fast becoming legendary. Where else, so far from civilisation, would one be offered a pre-dinner gin and tonic, mouth-watering barbecued venison steaks and port with one's coffee?

The fishing is good too! A 70% rainbow, 30% brown mix averaging 1 to 1.5kg with several double figure (lbs) fish taken each year. The fish are mainly wild stock and spectacular fighters. There are dozens of enticing pools within easy reach of the camp and all casting is done to sighted fish. So good spotting, stealth and presentation are all important.

Getting out involves a leisurely raft trip, fishing en route. Surprisingly Dave's tariffs are well within the reach of the average Kiwi — costs are all-inclusive. Not surprisingly, he gets a lot of repeat overseas business as well.

The area fishes best around February. The main river is open all year round but above the Taiuarau/Ngaruroro junction the season is 1 October to end April. Access to the middle reaches is very limited and always with the landowner's permission.

Dave Mabin is a strong advocate of catch and release and prefers the use of barbless hooks. He is a self-taught and highly practical fly tier. Some of his more popular patterns follow:

HALFBACK RABBIT
This effective hybrid utilises the tips of rabbit fur and is tied on a size 10 hook. Bound with very fine copper wire; tail of fine brown feathers.

OMAHAKI NYMPH
Tied on sizes 10 to 14 hooks. Dave has designed this nymph specifically to imitate naturals in the area. A particularly good rainbow trout pattern, it must be weighted.

RABBITS — GREEN & RED
Dave finds these great early and late season lures and for when the water is discoloured. The red marker seems to trigger a strong response from rainbows. On size 6 hooks, weighted.

HALFBACK MAGGOT
Another useful Ngaruroro fly. Weighted with fine copper wire on sizes 8 to 10 hooks. Pheasant tail, light tan polydub body and swannundaze halfback.

MABIN'S DRY
The Ngaruroro has some startling rises, some in the middle of the day. This simple but deadly dry fly is handy to have for such occasions. Body is of brown or black tying silk. Brown dry-fly hackle with tail two fine slips of pheasant tail or similar. Tied on 10 to 14 size hooks.

NGARURORO SPIDER
Amongst the myriads of naturals found in such a back-country river are the prolific water spiders. The body is formed with grey pantyhose and the legs with pheasant tail or hare's hair. Best on a size 12 hook or smaller.

TWILIGHT BEAUTY

SKIDDER

MARK'S SMELT

PHEASANT TAIL

BOATMAN

BLACK GNAT

HARE & COPPER

BASIL'S SMELT

Tukituki River, Hawkes Bay

This splendid trout river rises in the foothills of the Ruahine Range and flows for about 80 km to the Pacific Ocean at Haumoana. It is a river of great character with long peaceful stretches, fast rapids and deep pools. Rainbows and browns are both found in its waters. Some of the Tukituki is open for all-year fishing, namely where it passes the wildlife refuge for 8 km above Waimarama and downstream to the sea from S.H.50 Bridge. Otherwise the season is 1 October to 30 April.

The Tukituki has a mainly shingle base with some large papa rocks — as depicted above. The area of the painting is known as the Pump Pool, a popular spot for anglers. Fish in the Tuki average around 1½ kg with much larger specimens regularly caught.

Mark Sherburn is a young angler who has fished the Tukituki for years. During his time working at Craft and Hern Sports, Havelock North, he developed his talent as a tier. His recommendations for the Tuki follow:

TWILIGHT BEAUTY
A good fly to use during a Tukituki dun hatch — fished in the slow, shallow tail of pools. Mark always ties this pattern with two hackles, one of honey grizzle and the other black.

SKIDDER
In early summer myriads of brown beetles frequent the river. Later massive hatches of sedge are encountered. Both these events induce a feeding frenzy amongst the trout. This fly, fished on dusk or after dark, should be cast across and down the river and retrieved in a jerky, skidding fashion. Mark says you can both feel and hear the take! Deer hair body and natural brown tail.

MARK'S SMELT
Tied very sparsely on a small hook and fished in the lower reaches during spring, with a fast retrieve. Tied darker than most smelt flies to imitate the whitebait which develops a dark brown gut after a couple of days in the river. Brown swannundaze body with one turn of white hackle and a white tail.

PHEASANT TAIL NYMPH
An "old faithful" which fishes best during early and late summer dun hatches. Unweighted to float just below the surface film.

BOATMAN
During the hot summer months water boatmen (*Sigara* spp.), can be found amongst the green river weed in backwaters. Trout cruise the weed margins looking for such tasty morsels. Fished with a very slow but jerky retrieve on a floating line, Mark's version is tied with pheasant tail body and legs plus a wing case of blue-green mallard wing.

BLACK GNAT
Traditional old-world dry fly normally representing a mayfly or *ephemeroptera*. This particularly plump and tempting tie from Barry Stone could be taken by trout for a blowfly.

HARE AND COPPER NYMPH
Never leave home without some, says Mark! He landed (and released) over 20 good fish on a single Hare and Copper one day on the Tukituki. Tied on a 12 hook with three or four turns of lead wire, the "spring wine" tag makes the fly especially deadly.

BASIL'S SMELT
The common smelt (*Retropinna retropinna*) is often imitated by fly tiers. Here Basil Jackson has used a silver body, silver rib, and white rabbit wing topped with mallard.

BADGER PALMER

DEER HAIR

BROWN BEETLE

RAFFIA BUG

CREEPER

OLIVE NYMPH

HALF BACK VARIATION

Mangawhero River, Wanganui District

It is hard to imagine a more pleasant spot to fish than under the beautiful Raukawa Falls on the Mangawhero River. This scenic site is alongside the main Raetihi-Wanganui road with easy, if somewhat steep, access. The fishing here is especially good after a long dry spell when there is rain and the water starts to colour. The Mangawhero, which is open to anglers all year round, is prone to flooding in the winter months.

Fish are often difficult to locate at water level and "spotting" from a higher vantage point is recommended. Fish lie in the natural channels scoured out of the papa rock bottom or in the crevices under cliff faces. In summer weed and filament algae often makes fishing harder. November/December and February/March are the better months.

Alan Waites is one of the keenest anglers. Alan's selection for the Mangawhero follows:

BADGER PALMER
An easy to tie dry fly for still water sections. The light colour assists visibility especially when it is floated in the shade under willows.

DEER HAIR DRY
An excellent floater even in white water. Calf hair wings which can be dyed — yellow is a good colour — again to aid visibility. Tied on larger hooks this fly works well when the cicada are prevalent.

BROWN BEETLE
Alan's variation of this popular little dry fly. The deer hair body gives it terrific buoyancy. Trout relish a feast of beetles. Effective when the grass grub beetle is on the wing.

RAFFIA BUG BEETLE
Here Alan has used an under-tie of deer hair plus deer hair hackles. Makes the pattern easy to tie and another great floater. Beetles are terrestrial but inevitably some fall onto the water whilst swarming.

CREEPER
A good heavy nymph that works well in the faster runs, especially in colouring water. Tied on a curved hook with randomly trimmed deer hair.

OLIVE NYMPH
Excellent general purpose pattern. Swannundaze wing case and silver tinsel improves its durability.

HALFBACK VARIATION
Alan finds the Halfback nymph deadly on Mangawhero trout. However it is rather fragile. So he has "toughened" it up with a swannundaze wing case and copper-wire ribbing. By the sound of things, Alan's flies have to be prepared for regular assaults on their fragility!

OTHER USEFUL PATTERNS
Pheasant Tail and Hare and Copper nymphs.

Rangitikei River, Central North Island

The Rangitikei is one of the North Island's principal river systems. From pristine headwaters to the shingle flats of the lower river, it is a river of great beauty and changing character. The upper catchment area drains mostly native forest and the reaches flow over hard rock substrate (greywacke) making for some of the clearest waters to be found anywhere. The middle river (as featured in the scene above) flows over shingle bottom and through rich farmland, past great papa cliffs.

Both rainbow and brown trout are found throughout the river. The rainbow is migratory within the river system, maturing in the lower river and spawning in the upper reaches and tributaries.

This river is an extremely challenging one for fly fishers — the sheer size, depth and water clarity demand high standards of casting and presentation. Success is more often than not measured in terms of quality not quantity. The Rangitikei does produce some huge trout.

BLUE DUN MATUKA
This fly, which simulates an escaping baitfish is a variation on the famous matuka patterns — originally from New Zealand but now very popular in the States. Tied here by Tom Kemper.

GREEN HUMPY
One of the more common patterns used in the western U.S. This "hard to sink" fly is readily accepted by New Zealand trout, especially when manuka beetles or cicadas are on the wing. Tied by Tom Kemper.

DAVE'S HOPPER
Like the Humpy, a deer-hair terrestrial pattern. Originated by the famous American tier Dave

Whitlock. This large fly is sometimes used as a dropper because it floats so well and is highly visible. Tied by Tom Kemper.

Phil Steck is a year-round fishing guide who alternates between Jackson Hole, Wyoming and New Zealand. He loves the fly-fishing here and has adapted several U.S. patterns to suit N.Z. fishing conditions:

SPARKLE NYMPH
An impressionistic pattern imitating many species of N.Z. mayflies when tied in a variety of sizes and colours. The Antron dubbing material reflects light to simulate lifelike gills and legs.

LITTLE RAINBOW
Very effective on big rainbows in deep pools. When fished deep, on a short strip and stop retrieve, the marabou feather gives incredible life to this fly. Based on the Troth Bullhead, developed by U.S. tier Al Troth for Montana brown trout.

GIRDLE BUGGER
A combination of two American patterns — the Woolly Bugger and the Girdle Bug. A major source of the rubber legs is the under garment sometimes worn by women, hence the name! These legs impart an action which is irresistible, to brown trout especially.

OLIVE AND BLACK NYMPH
An easily-tied nymph used in sizes 12 to 16. Creates less of a fish-scaring "plop" when presented. Tied by Jack MacKenzie, it is ideal for slow, clearwater conditions.

RANGITIKEI STONEFLY
Another MacKenzie special, normally tied on a size 10 or 12 2X-long hook. Imitates the larger stoneflies and mayflies found on the river. Heavily weighter for deeper, faster runs, it is made from dubbed hare's mask, turkey quill, fine copper wire and soft black hackle with a latex wing case.

GINGER QUILL

PARTRIDGE & ORANGE

LUNKERBUSTER

RANKIN DRY

IRRESISTABLE

BLACK & PEACOCK

BLOODWORM

PALE QUILL

HARDY'S FAVOURITE

Mangatainoka River, near Pahiatua

If you want to have a lot of fun as well as great fishing, try to get to Pahiatua each October. Labour Weekend sees the annual Pahiatua Trout Fishing Carnival. With 200 kms of known fishing water, within half an hour's driving of this small provincial New Zealand town, it is no wonder it is such a popular event. Headquarters is located in a local restaurant. The place is jampacked each evening, with much discussion of the day's heroic encounters. Out-of-towners are often amazed at the quality of fish weighed in and always enjoy the friendly atmosphere that prevails.

The Mangatainoka (or "Toki" as it is affectionally known locally) River usually supplies the majority of fish taken. This is a wonderful river with trout that are known for their hard-fighting qualities. It is open all year up to the Hukanui Road bridge with (seasonal) fly fishing only above this. Access and wading is easy in most sections. The bag limit is 12 trout — easily sustainable with the prolific fish population currently. Many locals prefer to practice catch and release anyway. Fish, mainly wild browns with only a few rainbows, average from one to two kilos in weight, with larger specimens caught regularly.

Mangatainoka means "river of the native broom" (*Carmichaelia flagelliformis*) a plant now sadly very rare within its watershed. It flows mainly through gentle pastoral scenery.

An angler who knows the river well is Roy Cotter, long-standing president of the local anglers' club. Roy has fished all over New Zealand but still finds his home waters best. His top three flies for the "Toki" follow — a dry, a wet and a nymph.

GINGER QUILL
Roy designed this to imitate the common *Deleatidium vernale* and *D. myzobranchia* duns. Ginger cock tail and hackle. Stripped peacock herl quill for body. Grizzle hackle tips for wings. In sizes 16 or 18.

PARTRIDGE AND ORANGE SPIDER
Very effective used across and down, or greased and fished upstream to sedging trout. An antique pattern deserving more than obscurity. Orange wool or silk body with a gold ribbing. Partridge hackle. In size 14.

LUNKERBUSTER
Roy's all purpose nymph. Deer hair tail, black floss or tying-silk body, with fine copper-wire ribbing. Thorax of hare guard hairs over lead or copper wire. Turkey wingcase. In sizes 12 to 16.

RANKIN DRY
This Royal Wulff derivation was introduced to the area by a South African angler who made annual visits for 20 years. Several local anglers use it exclusively.

IRRESISTABLE
Doug Allen is another successful local angler. The name is not a misprint, for Doug finds his variation of the famous Irresistible most able for many situations. Fished large (in sizes 10 or 12) trout can't resist it.

BLACK AND PEACOCK
In sizes 12 to 16 fished across and down as a standard wet, or, as in this case, weighted with copper wire as a nymph.

BLOODWORM
Malcolm Shield has fished locally for nearly 20 years. He ties this simple ambush pattern in sizes 16 to 18.

PALE QUILL
In sizes 16 to 18 an excellent dry early season. Malcolm feels paleness is the key to its success.

HARDY'S FAVOURITE
A variation of a classic which Malcolm has come up with to fish to sedging trout. Tied fairly "fluffy" to keep hackle fibres as erect as possible when wet. Sizes 12 to 16.

Waiohine River, Wairarapa

The Wairarapa has several first-class trout rivers, the Waiohine included. Its upper reaches are in the magnificent Tararua Forest Park so one should be prepared to share the area with trampers from time to time. This section of the river runs through steep bush covered hills with several rugged gorges. There is good access from State Highway 2 just south of Carterton. The painting is of the Wall's Whare area between Totara Flats and the plain.

A river of very high water quality, it is fast flowing, tumbling through many boulder runs, with rock cover extremely abundant. There are good numbers of largish (1.5 to 3kg) resident brown trout throughout the upper reaches. Open to fishing all-year round, summer is the most favoured period. The low water levels and warmer water make access and wading easier and more comfortable.

In December 1988 the Wellington Acclimatisation Society released 500 yearling Ruakituri rainbows into the Waiohine. This was followed by 1000 in 1989 with another 1000 introduced in 1990. It is hoped that these fish, which come from an area of river blocked off to the sea by a waterfall, have developed river residency habits. Time will tell if the experiment works.

The artist's uncle, John Keedwell of Carterton, knows the river of old. After war service he returned to become manager of the Masterton trout hatchery. He remembers well one occasion when he took a famed Wellington angler, the late Bert Nimmo, to fish the area. A competent fisherman himself, John recalls how impressed he was with Bert's expertise. The first fly featured on this page has become a memorial to this fine angler.

NIMMO'S KILLER
Created by Bert Nimmo and used by him with great success. Body is of two sections — the rear half red floss and the forward portion black, ribbed with fine silver tinsel. In sizes 10 to 16. Tier: Garth Coghill.

DEER HAIR CADDIS
Lee Tan is a Wellington-based computer consultant. He loves the solitude of wilderness rivers such as the Waiohine. He finds this dry fly useful in slower water which has plenty of vegetation and cover.

PHEASANT TAIL
One of Lee's favourite flies, it imitates the mayfly nymphs found in Wairarapa waters. When tied with a slight hump and fished with movement, it also appears to be taken by trout for a water-boatman, which are prolific in this area.

Wayne Harter is an ex-American marine who stayed on to fish New Zealand after the Pacific campaign. He is secretary of the North Wairarapa branch of the Acclimatisation Society and a keen angler and fly tier. His recommended patterns for the Waiohine follow:

GOLDIE
A parachute-hackle dry which owes its ancestry, like its tier, to North America. Very effective on the Waiohine.

GRANDAD
Wayne uses his own hair, spun in and trimmed out, to produce this unusual fly. It is fortunate he has an ample supply of the raw product!

CICADAS
Two home-grown patterns to imitate the plump little insect noted for its high pitched chirping and remarkable turn of speed when disturbed. Recent long hot dry summers have meant a profusion of cicadas. Trout are extremely partial to them and it is an unwise angler who doesn't carry an imitation or two.

ADAMS
extended body

WILLOW GRUB

REID'S OLIVE

ANTRON
WING SPINNER

BLACK
NYMPH

RED TIPPED

GOVERNOR

TWILIGHT
BEAUTY

Ruamahanga River, Wairarapa

The Ruamahanga is Wairarapa's largest river, flowing from the Tararuas, down past Masterton and into Lake Wairarapa near Palliser Bay. Featured here is "The Cliffs" area near Masterton. This part of the Ruamahanga is of special delight to the angler. Within a few metres one can be casting to trout feeding on emerging insects in a pool, "ambushing" trout in one of the many backwater areas or "dapping" along the willow-lined banks.

Dapping, for the uninitiated is the art of gently lowering the fly onto the water as opposed to casting. It can be a particularly deadly form of fishing producing often hilarious antics on the part of a fish-following angler! Startling evening rises occur in this area. Author and angler Tony Orman says the best evening rise he has ever witnessed, was on the Ruamahanga.

Ninety-nine percent of the trout in the river are stream bred wild brown trout of at least 10 generations stock. Clark Reid, a local guide, maintains that the Wairarapa offers angling, in specific places, that will rival and indeed equal the great Southland fishery. In these days of rising transport costs this has to be good news for North Island anglers.

Clark, an accomplished fly tier too, has tied up five of his favourite Ruamahanga flies. You will note that these are all barbless for better penetration and release. Like most professional fly fishing guides these days, Clark is an adherent of "catch and release". Also included are a couple of more commercially available dry flies.

EXTENDED BODY ADAMS
An American dry fly pattern especially deadly during the *Deleatidium* spp. dun hatches on the Ruamahanga. It is imperative to use superior quality hackles thus ensuring maximum flotation. In size 16.

WILLOW GRUB
In mid-summer trout feed on the minute willow grubs which fall onto the water. This presents the angler with a real challenge. Clark uses a simple detached body of primrose Antron yarn with tip cemented slightly. In sizes 18 or 20.

REID'S OLIVE NYMPH
Variation of the popular U.S. pattern Lingren's Olive. Useful for back waters, ponds and placid margins. Tied marabou herl body, black ostrich herl thorax, grouse wing case and copper ribbing. Its secret seems to lie in the use of natural materials, imparting subtle life-like movement. In size 16.

ANTRON WING SPINNER
Best for *Deleatidium vernale* spinner falls — common in this area. Moose hair tail and pheasant tail body. In size 20.

BLACK NYMPH
Used for general daytime nymphing. A simple but effective pattern. In size 16.

RED-TIPPED GOVERNOR
A traditional dry fly presumed to be an American derivation of an old English pattern. From the vice of Basil Jackson, Rotorua. In size 14.

TWILIGHT BEAUTY
This pattern, also tied by Basil, imitates the spinner of *Coloburiscus humeralis* — a mayfly commonly found on warm Ruamahanga summer evenings. In size 12.

GREEN STONEFLY

PHEASANT TAIL var

PETERKEN'S POSSUM

GREEN NYMPH

CHEZ SPARKLE STONE

FRITTER

WHITEBAIT

Otaki River, Wellington District

The Otaki River rises high in the Tararua Ranges, flowing through mountain gorges until it is joined by tributaries at Otaki Forks. This is the area portrayed and is the limit of road access. The river then heads down through a gently-curving gorge onto the Horowhenua Plains and to the Tasman Sea.

It is a river of variety from mountain scenery, to wide gravel beds, to a sparkling sunlit gorge and finally to its estuary. Its fishing varies too, from mountain character to shingly bed, to the merging of the river with the surge of the Tasman's tide.

You will rarely see another angler on the Otaki — this solitude is a delightful attribute. The well-conditioned, but perhaps not numerous, brown trout in the river highlight the fine fishing that is available in the Wellington Acclimatisation Society District.

One angler who fishes the Otaki from time to time, rekindling boyhood memories from the fifties, is Tony Orman, author of some 14 outdoor books, among them trout-fishing titles such as the classic *Trout with Nymph* and its sequel *More Trout with Nymph*. Here are some Orman recommendations for the Otaki:

GREEN STONEFLY
A splendid pattern to use on the big bouldery water in the lower gorge. Good in any fast water, whether it is amongst the large boulders and aerated water, or down in the rapids and runs of the lower reaches.

PHEASANT TAIL VARIANT
For low summer conditions and quiet water, try a Pheasant Tail varied by a fur dubbing thorax. Can also be useful in fast water or on nymphing fish in quieter areas.

PETERKEN'S POSSUM
A lure developed by the late Syd Peterken of Waipukurau, a prominent Hawkes Bay angler of his day. This fly has proved effective in the lower reaches of many North Island rivers.

GREEN NYMPH
A neat and deadly nymph from Allan Rush. Quite often the simplicity of such a pattern will work wonders.

CHEZ SPARKLE STONE
Well-knwon American angler Jack Dennis came up with this beauty whilst fishing in New Zealand a couple of years ago. He added rubber legs to a size 8 stonefly pattern and had instant results. Fished dead drift or with slight twitch to impart life to the legs.

FRITTER & WHITEBAIT
Two patterns from Basil Jackson, designed to imitate *Galaxias maculatus* or whitebait. A food source much loved by trout and anglers alike! Basil excels when it comes to creating "practical" flies.

Hutt River, Wellington

Most Wellingtonians live in shameful ignorance of the fact that a remarkable trout river flows through their area. Where else in the world can the inhabitants of a capital city be fly fishing for wild trout within minutes of their homes?

Fishing in the Hutt River, in spite of modern man's savage depredations, is still extremely productive. A recent drift diving survey conducted by Steve Smith, field officer for the Wellington Acclimatisation Society, established a density of 100 trout per kilometre! As Steve says, not only is the river full of fish but it is under-used by anglers.

The Hutt is open all year round. A nice touch is that anglers under 12 years of age don't need a licence. The area featured is Maoribank Bridge in Upper Hutt suburbia.

Alan Cameron is a self-confessed fishing addict. He is past president and an active committee member of the Hutt Valley Angling Club. This is a progressive and enthusiastic band of anglers — well worth a beginner joining. Alan's special ties for the Hutt are:

THE HUTT G.P.
A fly Alan likes to use in the summer months, especially in the afterglow of sunset. Best cast towards the tail of a pool, into the smoother, slower water. G.P.? Golden Pheasant crest tail!

RED-TIPPED GOVERNOR NYMPH
Good during spring fishing — partlcularly on trout lurking amongst boulders in the shallows. Can be used weighted or unweighted.

BLACK POSSUM
Now we know what happens to all that fur on the road! A good general purpose nymph, generally better in smaller sizes (14 and 16). Black possum fur — abdomen clipped short, thorax left bushy.

Keith Collins is a parasitologist with a well-known chemical firm in Wellington. An Englishman by birth, Keith has fished since he was four. He began to tie flies at university and won first prize in the prestigious Veniard's "Swannundaze" fly-tying competition in 1979. His "specials" for the Hutt are:

HUTT RED SEDGE
A Collins' variant of the American Elk hair caddis. The head is finished to give an obvious head capsule unlike the U.S. pattern which has a tuft of deer hair. Fished on summer evenings; skated across the shallows at dusk when the trout are feeding on sedges.

CASEY'S NYMPH
A *Coloburiscus* imitation tied here on a specialist nymph hook. An "artform" pattern which certainly catches fish. Both this and the "Pearler" below were copied from naturals taken from the Hutt River by Keith in 1987.

THE "PEARLER" STONEFLY NYMPH
A complicated Collins' original best only attempted by accomplished tiers. Irresistible to opportunist feeders in late summer and autumn.

Traditional patterns suitable for the Hutt are:
Nymphs — Hare and Copper and Pheasant Tail. Wets — March Brown, Red-Tipped Governor and Scotch Poacher. Dries — Twilight Beauty, Blue Dun and:

KAKAHI QUEEN
An effective copy of *Ameletopsis percitus* — a mayfly common throughout New Zealand.

THE HUTT G.P.

RED TIPPED GOVERNOR nymph

BLACK POSSUM

HUTT RED SEDGE

CASEY'S NYMPH

THE PEARLER

KAKAHI QUEEN

DIPTERA EMERGER

MIDGE PUPA

MOLE FLY

BLUE DUN

CORIXA

ROYAL
HUMPY

HARE'S EAR
SPIDER

Wainuiomata River, Wellington

There are two excellent trout rivers that flow very close to New Zealand's capital city — the Hutt and the Wainuiomata. From its origins in the Rimutaka range, the Wainuiomata flows in a generally southern direction until it meets Cook Strait. It is untypical of the normal boulder bottom, fast-flowing North lsland rivers — being a low gradient, meandering river with a mainly sandy or silt substrate bottom.

Although there are about 35 kms of fishable water, it is the lower 10 kms which are most popular with anglers. Access is easy in most places, off the unsealed road which leads to the sea.

Slow water, high eroding banks and the large numbers of visible trout make it a challenging river to fish. The infamous Wellington breezes can also play havoc with casting — it is worth remembering that a light southerly makes for comfortable fishing. Good presentation, polaroid glasses and light gear are essential. Ultra-careful stalking of the easily spooked, cruising brown trout is called for, — an angler is quite likely to see 50 to 60 trout in a day.

The season is between 1 October and 30 April, with a four-fish bag limit. Exclusively brown trout, the average weight of a Wainuiomata fish is 1.5kg. Several 3kg plus fish are taken each year.

Some recommended patterns for the Wainuiomata:

KIMBALL'S *DIPTERA* EMERGER
This is a midge pattern much favoured by Jim Greeks of Wellington, for low water conditions in summer. When the fish are surface feeding and the traditional mayfly or caddis patterns are being ignored. Jim savours the extra challenge of fishing the Wainuiomata at this time. He ties these flies down to size 24 for extreme conditions.

MIDGE PUPA
Jim notes that midges are prevalent on the Wai-

nuiomata at times. This simple-to-tie pattern should be fished dead drift.

MOLE FLY
Another keen and equally successful local angler is John McDowall. He mainly fishes the river with a dry fly. This large bushy pattern, tied in sizes 8 to 14, is used when caddis are hatching — usually at dusk but often well into the night.

BLUE DUN
A smaller pattern, in sizes 14 and 16, used by John early in the season. Imitates *Deleatidium* spp duns.

CORIXA
Tied here by Mike Weddell of Dunedin, who in his book *Ten of the Best New Zealand Trout Flies*, devotes five pages to it. Mike is an Englishman, a former world casting champion and a devotee of fishing in this country. As he points out, stalking fish as they feed on waterboatmen can provide some real nerve-tingling action. In summer Wainuiomata browns cruise the slow weedy backwaters, gorging on these insects.

MANUKA ROYAL HUMPY
This is a fly developed and tied here by Jack Dennis, the well known American angling author and video maker. Jack fishes New Zealand waters as often as his busy schedule allows and this is a fly which works well for him here. The dyed green elk or deer hair makes this an excellent imitation of the manuka or green beetle.

HARE'S EAR SPIDER
One of the "Captain Hamilton's Famous Five" wet flies; productive now as it was in 1904 when Captain Hamilton wrote his angling classic *Trout Fishing and Sport in Maoriland*. This meticulous copy of the original was tied by Garth Coghill of Rotorua.

ANGLERS' PARADISE 73

Motueka River, Nelson District

SMITH'S BI-VISIBLE

KITE'S IMPERIAL

WILLOW WORM

GADDIS NYMPH

HORN CASED CADDIS

DARK COPPER

ORNATE MAYFLY

PASSIONFRUIT HOPPER

M.M. NYMPH

BLUE DARTER

ZULU

This splendid brown trout river and its tributaries form a gentle river system some 120km in length. From the Baton Bridge, in the beautiful and tranquil Motueka valley, there are good roads along both sides of the river to the sea at Motueka township. These afford good angling access in many places. The Motueka is a safe river to fish despite its good flow. It has an interesting variety of productive fishing water. The scene above portrays the area immediately below Baton Bridge. Here the river has a stable bed which makes the fishing so good. Some call this the best brown trout water in the South Island and certainly the evening rises can be spectacular!

Average fish are around a kilo but many are taken over this. Limit bag is 10 fish, with a minimum length of 30cm. Open season is from 1 October to 30 April.

S/Ldr A.G. Smith, a well known and respected Nelson angler, has spent many happy hours fishing and studying the Motueka. A selection of six of his flies for this river follow:

SMITH'S BI-VISIBLE
A well-proven pattern — should be lightly hackled for quiet water and heavier for rough stretches. On size 10 for broken water and down to 16 for low water on the flats.

WILLOW WORM
Trout feeding on the natural grub are very selective — normally having a beat just downstream of a willow. They will rise steadily and are not often startled. As the grub floats flat on the surface film, try to imitate this with the fly.

KITE'S IMPERIAL
A fly developed in England in 1962 and not often seen in New Zealand. It is however most effective when small mayflies are hatching.

CADDIS NYMPH
A good general purpose nymph pattern. Weighted with copper wire, then a body of light

grey wool ribbed with silver wire and given a light coat of clear varnish.

DARK COPPER
S/Ldr Smith finds this an extremely effective pattern. As with all nymph fishing a careful approach and accurate presentation are vital — so much depends on that first cast.

HORN CASED CADDIS
Imitates the common caddis *Olinga feredayi* — so often found in Motueka trout. The larvae have orange-brown heads and are about 10mm long. The trumpet-shaped horn case is chestnut-brown in colour.

PASSIONFRUIT HOPPER
Norman Marsh, well known author and angler, has settled on the banks of the Motueka. The first time he tried this pattern there it took four good trout each first cast! The natural is a common insect in this fruit-growing area. Tie this fly on 18 or 16 hooks, no smaller.

BLUE DARTER
Another Marsh design, developed from the Grey Darter mentioned in his classic *Trout Stream Insects of New Zealand*. The blue wing case is from the lovely blue-green speculum feather on a mallard duck wing. Tied in sizes 16 to 12.

ORNATE MAYFLY
Peter Schasching's innovative imitation of the *Nesameletus* spp. a mayfly common to most NZ rivers. It is a fast, erratic swimmer.

MM NYMPH
("MARSHALL'S MONSTROSITY")
Developed by Graeme Marshall, an experienced fishing guide who lives on the Motueka. Graeme, together with Les Hill, co-authored *Stalking Trout* — another NZ classic.

ZULU
The editor of *NZ Fisherman*, Bill Kirk, ties this old English pattern for rivers such as the Motueka. It successfully simulates a hatching insect about to escape the water.

ADAMS

MAYFLY DUN

MAYFLY SPINNER

HORN CADDIS NYMPH

MAYFLY NYMPH

MAHOGANY ELK HAIR CADDIS

LEAF HOPPER

PHEASANT TAIL

Spring Creek, Blenheim

This delightful stretch of water near Blenheim is one of New Zealand's fly-fishing gems. Several overseas anglers, for example, make lengthy annual pilgrimages to fish it exclusively. One major American fishing magazine has called it "one of the world's best dry fly streams". However, there are flies in the ointment as well as on the water . . . Spring Creek is in dire need of sensible management policies and is a prime candidate for a "Local Conservation Notice" to implement these.

Spring Creek flows tranquilly through horticultural land and willows. It has clear water even when other local rivers are unfishable. It is slightly colder than other waters in the district. This plus the plentiful cover available makes it a superb brown trout habitat. Often as deep as it is wide, it is deceptively fast flowing. Ultra careful stalking and presentation is vital; providing that challenge so beloved by trout anglers.

There is easy access upstream of the State Highway 1 bridge just north of Blenheim. Otherwise fishing is with land owners' permission only. Most are very accommodating to true fly fishermen.

Average fish are 1.5 to 2 kg, with many larger fish taken. Season is 1 October to end of April. Bag limit is 4 trout. Spinning is currently permitted.

If ever there was a case for a purely fly fishing area this must be it — one could be braver and even suggest it becomes a "catch and release" fishery. This would greatly enhance its value to the district.

Another undoubted asset to the area is Timara Lodge. This lovely old homestead set in beautiful surroundings is owned and run by Rosemary and Graham Sutton. Luxurious accommodation, fine local food and wines, plus friendly hospitality makes this a great base for visiting anglers.

Geoff Robinson, a local pharmacist and Spring Creek addict, has tied these five flies especially for this page:

ADAMS
An internationally-popular dry fly which originated in the States circa 1892. Its general resemblance to mayflies must account for its success on Spring Creek.

MAYFLY DUN
Similar to Dad's Favourite but tied with clear wings. These wings are formed from unwound synthetic string.

MAYFLY SPINNER
The low-lying silhouette of this polywing spinner fools even the most selective of Spring Creek browns.

HORN CADDIS NYMPH
Weighted to reach the deep feeders. Geoff suspects it is also taken for a mayfly nymph. Tied to represent the larva.

MAYFLY NYMPH
Similarly weighted with a lead under-body and copper over-body. *Ephemeroptera* (mayflies), especially their nymphs, are an important source of food for Spring Creek trout.

MAHOGANY ELK HAIR CADDIS
Richard Abrams from Chicago is a regular visitor. This fly is one of several he has especially tied for his New Zealand forays. The tier is Al Troth; originator of this pattern. The fly is coloured mahogany, here, to imitate the leaf hopper found in the area.

LEAF HOPPER
A more exact copy of the real thing. On windy days these insects are blown into the water, where cruising browns avidly devour them. Tier: Al Troth (Montana).

PHEASANT TAIL
Well known angling authority Tony Orman loves to fish Spring Creek when his busy schedule allows. His variant (using greenstone wool) of this nymph is Tony's first choice. Refer to Speckled Nymph in his excellent book *Trout with Nymph*.

Upper Wairau River, Marlborough

The Wairau River rises in the high mountain ranges and flows north-westwards through Rainbow Station, spreads across the Wairau Valley, often in a series of channels, and finally enters the ocean near Blenheim. About 100 kilometres up-river from Blenheim the river becomes known as the Upper Wairau; a quiet beautiful stretch of water which maintains a healthy population of large brown trout. Open season is from 1 October to 30 April with a bag limit of four fish upstream of the Wash Bridge.

Tony Entwistle, a Nelson-based professional fly fishing guide, often takes his overseas and New Zealand clients to the Upper Wairau. He also enjoys fishing it for pleasure. When on its banks everything seems right with the world — however it isn't! The Marlborough Power Board proposes building a power scheme on this precious river, starting at the 5-mile confluence. Research has shown that 50% of Wairau trout spawn above this point. The effects of a scheme such as this on trout stocks throughout the river, water quality and underground water tables, are too dismal to even contemplate. Needless to say local anglers are up in arms and (at the time of writing) the Marlborough Anglers were seeking a Conservation Order for the Upper Wairau. All power to their efforts.

GREY DUN
A general mayfly imitation, especially useful for those midday dun hatches, tied upside-down to ensure greater acceptability to selective Wairau browns. In sizes 10-14. Designed and tied by Tony Entwistle.

RED GILL
An attractor nymph for those difficult days when conditions conspire against success. Useful early season or after rain, when the Wairau takes on the classic milky blue hue of southern glacier-fed rivers. Size 10, weighted. Another Entwistle original.

PETE'S PARACHUTE
This low-floating, extended-body, parachute mayfly imitation is especially effective later in the day — when trout selectivity increases. Best in sizes 12 or 14. Designed and tied by Peter Carty.

GRIZZLY KING TRUDE
Popular American pattern imitating many terrestrials, including cicadas which are common on the Wairau during hot windy mid-summer afternoons. Long shank hook in sizes 10 or 12. Tied by Peter Carty.

GREEN STONEFLY
A brown trout staple during early season, especially in the boisterous rocky runs or at the heads of pools. This is Peter Carty's variation and is one of the most effective. Long shank hook in sizes 8 or 10, weighted.

YELLOW CADDIS
Late in the season, yellow flies seem to trigger the best response in Wairau trout. This caddis variation, designed and tied by David Moate, works well in the deeper runs and riffles. Weighted and with the assistance of a microshot or two, it gets close to the bottom. Partridge Shrimp hook in sizes 10-14.

GROUSE AND PURPLE
A variant of the soft-hackle flies so popular late last century. This weighted Moate design fishes well to edgewater or tailwater trout. Partridge Shrimp hook in sizes 10-14, weighted.

THE MACKAY FLY
Specifically tied to simulate a small black cranefly-type insect which is prolific on the Wairau in the early to mid season. The white tuft improves visibility and the splash of orange helps focus the trout's attention. In size 12. Designed and tied by Ron Mackay.

Mangles River, Nelson Lakes

HARE & COPPER

GRAY AFTY

MAC'S NYMPH

GOOSEBERRY NYMPH

OLIVE STONEFLY

ADAMS parachute

The Nelson Lakes area is one of great scenic beauty. Tony Entwistle (Nelson Lakes Guiding Services) can offer his clients a choice of over 30 fishable rivers.

Some of these rivers are extremely vulnerable to increased pressure or "fish hog" tactics. Tony and his team of guides specialise in "catch and release" using only barbless hooks. It is reassuring to see professional guides actively promoting conservation of a fragile resource, whilst managing to make a success of utilising it.

We asked Tony for a "small-water selection" to cover this type of fishing. He and Ron Mackey tied up the following:

HARE AND COPPER NYMPH
No selection would be complete without this nymph. It is successful in sizes 16-8 and can be either heavily weighted or not weighted at all, depending on water conditions. There is a big difference between a well-tied Hare and Copper and a poorly-tied one — the fly should taper from head to tail and should be quite bulky. The speckled guard hairs should stick out all over the fly, giving the impression of life, legs and movement. This fly represents many forms of sub-aquatic life and this is probably the main reason for its success.

GRAY AFTY NYMPH
A real charmer, the secret of this fly is in the soft and supple hackle that seems to breathe life. This fly was developed during the low-water conditions late in the 1984/5 season when fishing was very tough and the trout super selective. In many cases this was the only fly fish would accept. It imitates emerging mayfly species and various caddis pupae. In sizes 14 and 12.

MAC'S NYMPH
Developed in the 1985/6 season when it looked as if another low-water spell was approaching. This never in fact eventuated but the fly proved a major success. The thin profile and weighted body ensures a fast sink rate. When you need to get the fly down quickly with as little splash as possible, Mac's Nymph is most useful. In sizes 14 and 12.

GOOSEBERRY NYMPH
Developed during the low-water conditions of the 1983/4 season, this fly is terrific on the selective fish found in the shallower riffle water. Fished on a fine tippet this fly will entice most feeding fish, even when the water is very low and clear. Sizes 18-14.

OLIVE STONEFLY NYMPH
A variation on the tried and true Green Stonefly. With the slimmer profile and slight change in colour this not only represents the *Stenoperla prasina* stonefly but also most of the larger mayfly species found in the Nelson district. Fished unweighted, it can be useful on most fish in moving water situations. When weighted it is ideal for deeper and swifter water and for when the rivers are slightly discoloured. Size: long shank 12.

ADAMS (PARACHUTE PATTERN) DRY FLY
One of Tony's favourite flies. It seems that most fish feeding on the surface will accept an Adams in sizes 16 or 14. The parachute pattern aids delicate presentation and shows more of the fly body to the trout. The grey-brown toning is very representative of many adult mayfly species.

Lake Brunner Lodge

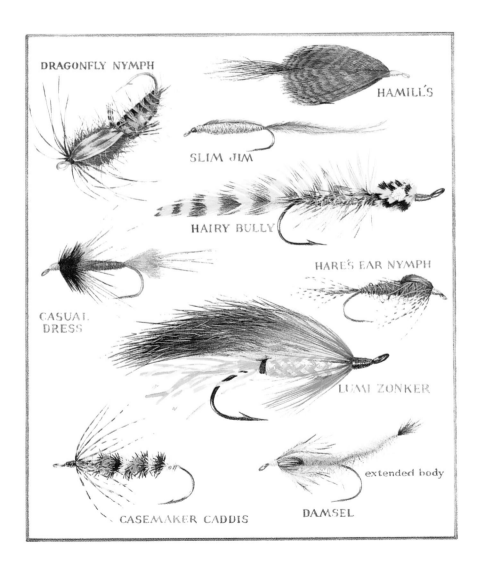

DRAGONFLY NYMPH

HAMILL'S

SLIM JIM

HAIRY BULLY

HARE'S EAR NYMPH

CASUAL DRESS

LUMI ZONKER

CASEMAKER CADDIS

DAMSEL

extended body

Lake Brunner, Westland

The West Coast of New Zealand's South Island is an area of great beauty and solitude. Human presence is dwarfed by lush native forests and magnificent glaciated mountains. It has a relatively high rainfall and consequently trout waters in profusion.

Lake Brunner is a gem of a lake — only $2^{1}/_{2}$ hours interesting driving from Christchurch. It has a predominantly brown trout population averaging around the 2 kg mark and is open to anglers all year round. Great sport is to be had ambushing cruising browns along the lake margins. Light tackle, a floating line and long leaders are recommended. Seeing a voracious fish approach and take your fly is heart-pounding stuff! Lake Brunner has good access in many places, to sandy white beaches interspersed with weed beds. There is also excellent river fishing in the vicinity. Bag limit is six trout, of which only one may be a rainbow.

Lake Brunner Lodge is one of the country's longest established fishing lodges. Lovingly restored by Marion van der Goes and Ray Grubb, it now must rate as one of New Zealand's finest. Overseas and New Zealand guests enjoy fine food, tranquil surroundings, exciting fishing and each other's company. Bruce Robertson is the Lodge's resident guide. When he's not guiding, he's fishing! As he says, "A perfect job . . ." The Lake Brunner fly selection:

DRAGONFLY NYMPH
Martin Langlands (formerly of the Tackle Box, Christchurch) used to tie most of the Lodge's flies. This "upside-down" nymph is keeled to sit hook up — thus avoiding snags and weed. Ideal Brunner-edge pattern.

HAMILL'S KILLER

North Island standard lure tied here by Steven Willis — a regular contributor tier to our calendars. A Hamill's on an 8 or even 10 size hook is useful at Brunner.

SLIM JIM

Bruce Robertson's Brunner smelt imitation. Of Antron and ostrich construction it regularly fools the patrolling browns. You'll note that Bruce sets his clients a good example with the use of barbless hooks. The Lodge encourages and promotes "catch and release".

HAIRY BULLY

Steven's favourite night fly originates from a Canterbury pattern, the Woolly Bully.

CASUAL DRESS

A Polly Rosborough (U.S.) original. Utilising muskrat fur and ostrich feather it "breathes" realistically on a slow retrieve. Produces some smashing strikes for Bruce's clients.

HARE'S EAR NYMPH

Bruce's favourite fly; partridge tail and hare's ear throat hackle.

LUMI ZONKER

U.S. pattern good for both harling and night fishing. Martin Langlands uses luminous flashabou tubing and rabbit fur.

CASEMAKER CADDIS

Martin's representation of a common local insect. Soft hackle for legs, with several different hackles (can be varied to suit habitat) wound around hook and trimmed.

EXTENDED BODY DAMSEL

Steven Willis has used marabou tail and leg fibres to give this fly fantastic action in the water.

ALI'S FLASHBACK

HORNED CADDIS

BLUE DUN

ROYAL WULFF var.

WILLOW GRUB

male

PHEASANT TAIL DRY

female

KAKAHI QUEEN NYMPH

KAKAHI PRINCE

La Fontaine Stream, Westland

Said by many to be the finest fly-fishing water on the West Coast. It is a tributary of the Big Wanganui River and rises in a swamp near the township of Harihari. Over the first 8km it meanders through farm land where it has been widened for drainage purposes. It is this section (as featured) that provides some of the best fishing for competent casters. This is a true "spring creek" — with gin-clear water, a gentle flow and deep pools. Weed makes casting difficult in places and the streambanks are often quite boggy. However, access is easy from the network of small roads that criss-cross the La Fontaine Valley. Ensure landowners' permission is gained where necessary.

Ali Thompson and Lynn Tapsell operate Mockingbird Hill Outfitters, based just south of Harihari. Ali, an ex-helicopter hunter and ultra keen all-round angler, now specialises in guiding clients on alpine hunting safaris for world-class thar and chamois. In addition he takes them fly fishing. The La Fontaine is a favourite but Ali says there are literally dozens of other spring creeks, streams and rivers in the district — all of which hold brown trout. Salmon and rainbows are also available nearby. One gathers, talking to Ali, that this is his Utopia!

The season is from 1 November to 30 April with early season giving the best fishing. There is downstream lure fishing, when the fish are pursuing whitebait, also nymphing and — best of all for Ali — superb dry-fly fishing. Being a spring creek the La Fontaine is not prone to the regular flooding experienced on the Coast. It is, though, vulnerable to angling pressure and thus practising catch and release is vital for its future.

ALI'S FLASHBACK
A novel variation of the popular nymph which Ali finds works well throughout the day.

HORNED CADDIS
Tied to imitate *Pycnocentrodes* spp, a caddis commonly found in the area. In his excellent book *Trout with Nymph*, Tony Orman devotes a full chapter to fishing with cased caddis imitations.

BLUE DUN
Ali Thompson delights in presenting a dry fly to La Fontaine browns. This traditional pattern imitates the natural blue duns *Deleatidium lillii*.

ROYAL WULFF VARIATION
Named for its originator Lee Wulff, well-known American fly tier, this is a popular dry fly throughout New Zealand. Ali's version is most successful in West Coast streams.

WILLOW GRUB
This outsized copy of the real thing (*Pontania proxima*) induces a vigorous response in La Fontaine trout in high summer. As the natural grows to only 6mm these fish must be eternal optimists!

COGHILL'S PHEASANT TAIL — male & female
Garth Coghill's rendition of New Zealand's most widely distributed mayfly *Coloburiscus humeralis* — the spiny gilled mayfly. After mating, the females fly low over the water, washing off the bright orange egg mass as they do so. Garth has often felt this orange colouring attracts the trout.

MARSH'S KAKAHI QUEEN NYMPH & KAKAHI PRINCE
Noted angling author Norman Marsh is a regular and enthusiastic visitor to the La Fontaine. Like Garth, he too recognises the importance of *C. humeralis* in this river. He designed the two flies illustrated to represent the nymph and adult (dun) stages in this prolific insect's life cycle. For more on these fascinating flies and the naturals see Norman's classic reference book *Trout Stream Insects of New Zealand*.

Lake Emily, Ashburton Lakes

There are 12 lakes of various sizes in the basin that lies between the headwaters of the Rakaia and Rangitata rivers, only two hours pleasant drive from Christchurch. Each of these diverse lakes has its own particular features and attractions. They nestle in wonderful "big country" with tawny tussock-covered mountains close-by and a backdrop of higher snow-clad mountains in the distance. Since they lie in the bottom of a wide glaciated basin the lakes are shallow and have extensive wetlands on their margins. Perfect wildlife habitat . . .

The Southern Crested Grebe is a unique and special bird. It is also an endangered one. This sub-species was first recorded in this country in 1846 by Charles Heaphy. A completely aquatic bird it is now in danger of extinction — there are estimated to be only 250 Crested Grebes in New Zealand! Their numbers have decreased in direct ratio to the development of the back-country lakes — in other words their habitat is being destroyed.

However the grebe and other species in this area have a knight in shining waders on their side! A remarkable and tenacious man, Jim Ackerley of Ashburton, is devoting his retirement years to saving the area from further "development". He had already been awarded a Conservation Citation by the N.Z. Nature Conservation Council, in recognition of his unstinting work in protecting this unique area. He is secretary of the local "Save the Rivers" organisation, a conscience group which lobbies all branches of government.

Jim Ackerley is also an ardent fly fisherman and an authority on the fishing locally. One of his favourite lakes is Emily — a smallish rather ordinary looking piece of water. It is however probably the best fontinalis fishery in the Southern Hemisphere, a fact attested to by the American anglers who make the effort to fish it. *Salvenus fontinalis*, the American brook trout, is in fact a char. Introduced to Emily in the late 1930's the fish there have developed a hump back and deep body quite unlike fontinalis elsewhere in New Zealand. They have also grown larger; to 3 kg plus, which is exceptional.

Despite all this Jim is concerned that Lake Emily could be destroyed in a plan to flood the surrounding basin — no doubt for some eminently practical purposes. Fortunately for Emily we have people like Jim Ackerley who will actively resist such irreversible vandalism of our natural heritage.

Open season is 1 November to the end of April for the lakes and it starts a month earlier for local rivers. While there is public access to most waters in the area, access to some is at the runholder's discretion. A 4WD vehicle is useful. Jim Ackerley's two recommended patterns for Emily follows:

EMILY EMERGER
A nymph he ties especially to tempt the chary char. Best time to fish the lake is at change of light.

BLOWFLY
Black deerhair and dyed pukeko substitute makes this a very useful fly for all the lakes in the district.

CLEARWATER DRY
From Derek Smitheram, a veteran and highly successful Emily angler. Developed by him for use on all these high-country lakes.

EMMA DAMSEL
Lake Emma, sister to Emily, contains exclusively brown trout. This Smitheram fly works well on the "fonties" too.

MOUSE
Derek keeps this for those days where nothing else seems to work. The appearance of a rodent has been known to interest shore-patrolling fontinalis.

WASP
Jim Tonkin ties up this pattern utilising pheasant tail plus black and blue floss.

NEV'S FANCY
A highly successful night lure from Neville Adams, another Ashburton angler. Neville received a Conservation Citation at the same time as his friend Jim Ackerley.

DENNY CADDIS
From Robert Wright, who used possum for the thorax, a peacock herl body and turkey feathers. Named for Lake Denny.

DRAGONFLY NYMPH
Robert finds this effective when the naturals are in evidence. Tied with green chenille and copper ribbing.

EMILY EMERGER

EMMA DAMSEL

CLEARWATER DRY

NEV'S FANCY

WASP

BLOWFLY

MOUSE

DENNY CADDIS

DRAGONFLY NYMPH

Lake Mapourika, South Westland

Most visitors to New Zealand comment on the diversity of its scenery. The West Coast of the South Island is certainly unlike any other part of the country. Where else in the world, for example, do rain forests exist alongside moving glaciers? The stunning mountain vistas and the serenity of Westland lakes are enchanting. True it has been known to rain (5,000 millimetres or 200 inches each year) but this is more than offset by the mild and often sunny climate.

Lake Mapourika, glacier-formed some 12,000 years ago, nestles in verdant bushland near the township of Franz Josef. Translated literally the name means "Flower of the Dawn" in Maori — symbolic of this water as the early morning mist is almost magical — mist rising, majestic mountain peaks coming into view and numerous signs of fish rising across the lake. In fact the lake was named by gold miners after a ship which plied the Sydney-New Zealand run.

Mapourika holds a good population of brown trout, resident Atlantic salmon, and around March each year sea-run quinnat salmon enter the lake. The season is from 1 October to 31 March for salmon and to 30 April for trout. Bag limit is 6 trout and 1 salmon daily.

The scene above depicts one of the lake's best fly-fishing spots. This is adjacent to both the MacDonald Stream inlet and Okarito River outlet. A stealthy early morning approach is advocated as the fish come in almost to the shoreline of the shallow beach.

Stan Peterson and his wife Myrna operate Westland Guiding Services. Stan caters for both alpine hunting and fishing clients. He also loves to fish Mapourika, as is evident from the fish on his trophy wall. Visiting anglers too will be captivated by this lovely lake. Some examples of flies useful in Mapourika are:

DOROTHY
Stan Peterson's top trout and salmon lure. A traditional fly which is best at change of light. Can be used for casting to smelting fish and for harling.

BLACK AND PEACOCK
One of author Mike Weddell's "ten best New Zealand trout flies". Mike ties this especially for flat, calm conditions, to catch slow cruising trout feeding on lake-edge snails. Although primarily a stillwater snail imitation, it does also make a reasonable representation for other trout food forms such as small black beetles.

MIDGE PUPA
Also a successful Weddell stillwater pattern is this midge pupa, which simulates the prolific chironomid or "non-biting" natural. Mike has found this fly very successful for trout that come close inshore, such as in the situation pictured above.

DOLL FLY
An American lure pattern which is high on Stan Peterson's list of essential Mapourika flies. Dressings can be varied widely but this one seems to work well in the lake.

MELLOW YELLOW
Lake Mapourika's dark water is a consequence of rainwater leaching through the forest floor. Christchurch angler and fly tier, John Morton, has devised this unusual creation to cater especially for these conditions. Fishing from a "belly boat" off Red Jack's Creek (another prime fishing spot on the lake), John took a brace of "the biggest browns I've ever seen".

CRAIG'S KILLER
This green lure tied Craig's-style by John Morton works well at the Okarito River outflow especially. John has also taken good quinnat salmon with it at dawn, fished deep. Named after its originator, Craig Adams.

BLACK GNAT
Stan Peterson recommends this traditional dry fly on Mapourika, early morning and late evening. Mark Sherburn's tying, featured here, is a particularly enticing one.

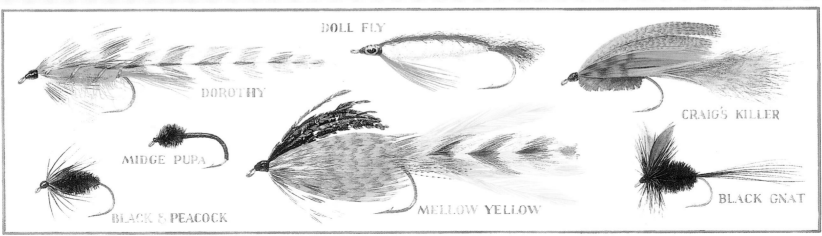

DOLL FLY

DOROTHY

CRAIG'S KILLER

MIDGE PUPA

BLACK & PEACOCK

MELLOW YELLOW

BLACK GNAT

Lake Alexandrina, South Canterbury

A clearwater lake which is claimed by many anglers to be the most productive stillwater fishing in the South Island. It certainly is a very high quality fishery with brown trout, rainbow trout and quinnat salmon. It is also a refuge for the uncommon Southern Crested Grebe *(Podiceps cristatus)* and has in fact, the largest population of these birds in any one New Zealand location. This, plus other wildlife on the lake, makes Alexandrina a superb place to enjoy the great outdoors.

Open season is from the first Saturday in November to 30 April. Bag limit is set at six acclimatised fish with a minimum length of 25 cm. Late season fishing produces some of the better catches.

The area featured is known as the "Pothole", a productive deep hole, especially good at night. Look out for cruising browns around the lake edge here too. Great care must be taken in this area as much of the edge is afloat on a raft of swampgrass! Don't head for the northern end of this lake in a norwester — it spoils the fishing.

Barry Stone is a Timaru butcher with a soft spot for Alexandrina. He is also an accomplished fly tier and here are three of his patterns for the lake.

PETE'S PRAYER
Tied to represent dragon fly larvae. Barry says that the smaller size of his imitation seems to fool the trout. Named after a friend who was found on his hands and knees frantically searching for a lost prototype, having caught several fish on it earlier.

MUDDLER MINNOW
Barry's variation of this famous U.S. pattern includes brown marabou which gives the lure plenty of life. Fished on a fast-sinking line.

CADDIS NYMPH
Casting to a cruising trout and raising the rod slightly as the fish approaches has been the key to Barry's success with this fly. Green swannundaze, varnished mallard quill wings, peacock herl head and brown partridge legs. On a size 14 caddis hook.

John Hayes is a scientist currently working at the Fisheries Research Centre, Rotorua. Lake Alexandrina's unique fishery formed the basis for his PhD thesis so he knows the area intimately. Two of his favourites:

PHIL'S BLOWFLY
Originated by a Canadian professor friend, especially for our high country waters. Dyed black deer hair makes it float like a cork. Blue lurex and squirrel tail for wings.

ORANGE WITCH
An attractive lure which could imitate the native koura *(Galaxias brevipinnis)* found in the lake. Remarkably there are no smelt present. This pattern utilises the barred flanks of the chukor, a high country game bird.

Peter Shutt of Timaru is a man of many parts: angler, fly tier, writer, guide, Acclimatisation Society stalwart and fervent promoter of South Island angling. His book *Fishing in the South Island* is a must for travelling anglers. Peter's offerings for Alexandrina are:

HALFBACK NYMPH
With case of florist paper. Heavily weighted and used on a floating line with long leader. Size 12 in the day, 8 at night.

MRS SIMPSON LURE
Called Kilwell No. 1 in the North Island. Fished deep on a sinking line. Size 8 in the day, size 4 in the evening.

UPSIDE-DOWN FLY (DRY)
Florist paper acts as a sail imparting natural movement to the fly. Sizes 12-16, depending on the surface ripple.

PETE'S PRAYER

PHIL'S BLOWFLY

MRS SIMPSON

HALFBACK NYMPH

MUDDLER MINNOW

CADDIS NYMPH

ORANGE WITCH

UPSIDE-DOWN FLY

Ahuriri River, Waitaki Valley

The upper Ahuriri is not what one would expect of a South Island high-country river — it is a big, smooth-gliding, somewhat meandering stretch of water. The basin it flows through once held a lake restrained by a large moraine. Eventually a gap was forced through this, forming this splendid river. It is a peaceful and beautiful area. Most anglers who frequent it do so as much for the solitude and surroundings as for the chance to catch a large trout.

The Ahuriri has grassy banks and easy access from the metal road which follows the river up this dramatic valley. Access permission should be obtained from the two stations in the area Ben Avon and Birchwood. This section of the Ahuriri holds a small population of often large trout. Average size is between 1.5 and 4 kg with trophy fish a distinct possibility for the competent angler. These fish get big because they are hard to catch! Skilled and careful presentation of the fly is vital on this river. Rainbows seldom venture above Ben Avon but browns are to be found throughout the length of the river.

In this section (upstream of the confluence with Longslip Creek) the bag limit is a sensible 2 fish. The season opens here first Saturday in December, running through to the end of April. Below Longslip Creek the bag limit is 5 fish and the season opens a month earlier. Artificial bait only throughout.

GRAND HAIR FLY

Local fishing guide Frank Schlosser loves the area. He is a highly regarded fly tier — this adaptation of a Wulff-style fly is a favourite of his for the Ahuriri. Tied with white calf tail wings, black wool body and two brown hackles.

POSSUM NYMPH

Frank uses grey possum fur and paradise duck wing feathers on this. A keen wildfowler he has no problems with materials! When he lived and guided on the Tongariro, Frank became well known for his nymphs, particularly the Flashback.

BUCK CADDIS

This yellow-bodied fly has a sika deer back and grey grizzle hackles. Frank finds it useful in the Ahuriri.

MAYFLY EMERGER

Young Christchurch tier Steve Willis always manages to come up with an original pattern. Steve recently took (and released) a 4 kg brown trout on it. Brown hen fibre tail, brown Antron/hare mix body, copper wire ribbing, brown hen hackle and dyed brown poly-wing wingcase.

UNDERTAKER

Peter Schasching is a friend of Steve's and another innovative young fly tier. He trained under Martin Langlands at Christchurch's well known "Tackle Box" — the specialist fly fishing store. Peter's remarkable creation is designed to look like several courses in one, to a foraging trout!

MORTON'S ANT

From that doyen of New Zealand fly tiers, John Morton. This "little tickler needs a pilot's licence to operate but it does go down very fast and prompts some exciting takes from the bigger bottom feeders as is my wont to chase these days". Imitates the blacky-green ants found in late summer.

ROYAL WHISKER

Originally designed as a high floater for western U.S. waters, this particular fly has been refined slightly by visiting Seattle angler Keith Simpson. He has used it successfully from Kashmir to Kenya but also to great effect on the Ahuriri. Tied with three hackles it sits high on the water.

LOOP-WING DUN

Another regular visitor to our waters is the well known American angling authority Gary Borger. He fell in love with the South Island's high-country fishing even making a video on the subject (*South Island Sampler*). Gary's Loop-Wing Dun provides a strong wing silhouette with a minimum of material.

GREEN CICADA

Considered one of the best cicada imitations around — from the vice of Brian Hussey, a top Taupo fishing guide and fly tier. Body is a closed cell foam or deer hair clipped to shape and then coloured with a felt pen. Reversed hackle wing. Head is clipped deer hair. Best in hook sizes 6 to 10.

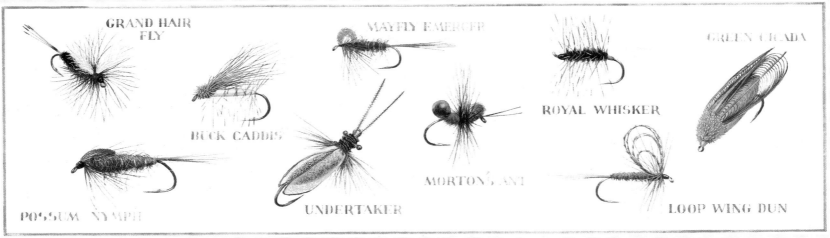

GRAND HAIR
FLY

MAYFLY EMERGER

GREEN CICADA

BUCK CADDIS

ROYAL WHISKER

POSSUM NYMPH

UNDERTAKER

MORTON'S ANT

LOOP WING DUN

Hakataramea River, South Canterbury

The earliest introductions of trout and salmon to New Zealand were made in this river — brown trout in the 1870's and rainbows in the early 1900's. These flourished and soon spread throughout the catchment. In 1900 a government hatchery was established on the Hakataramea to initiate a sea-run stock of quinnat and sockeye salmon. Indeed the Waitaki area soon became a famous salmon fishery. Sadly the construction of several hydro dams has since severely affected this. Quinnat salmon are now restricted to the lower Waitaki area only.

Normal season is 1 October to 30 April with artificial fly only allowed on the Hakataramea. A copy of the local regulations should be obtained to ascertain the varying bag limits etc. The "Haka" is at its best early in the season but the clarity of its water means careful presentation is vital.

Graeme Warren is a keen Haka and Waitaki angler. He is also deeply concerned that proposed further hydro works will destroy what is still superb recreational fishing. His 'Save the Waikati' petition deserves full support.

GRAEME'S CADDIS
A Warren speciality — he uses natural moth cocoon wings and hare's fur. At times a magical taker of trout.

BLACK FLY
Barry Cooke is a noted Irish artist and keen fly fisherman. Recently he was Graeme Warren's fishing guest and whilst in the area tied up this successful little beauty.

MUSKRAT
Graeme Hughes has been the local Waitaki Valley Acclimatisation Society's field officer for 25 years and can safely be said to know the Haka well! He was intrigued by the action muskrat fur has under water and developed this fly as a result. A great change-of-light pattern.

BROWN MAYFLY
Tied from an old sheepskin on Graeme's office chair! Represents *Deleatidium myzobranchia*, a mayfly common to the area.

GREEN STONEFLY
Tied by Graeme to imitate the early season stonefly *Stenoperla prasina*. An attractive and effective pattern especially on rainbows.

WAITAKI SEDGE
This "flymph" is designed to be fished sub-surface or in the surface film. Graeme feels that the untidier it is the better! Really deadly at night when caddis are moving.

PINK ATTRACTOR
Omarama fishing guide Frank Schlosser is well known for his innovative and practical patterns. Finding fish rising to his pink strike indicator one day, Frank tied this fly up out of a similar coloured yarn.

GREEN CADDIS LARVA
A more conventional but equally effective Schlosser fly.

DAMSEL FLY
A delightful tie from Noel Thomas of Temuka. Noel became known as a skilled dry-fly tier during his many years as a tackle retailer.

COCKSEDGE
This fly was originally tied for the Goodradigbee River near Canberra by Chris Hole, an ex-Australian Navy captain, angling artist and keen fisherman. Chris makes an annual pilgrimage to the South Island and has found that his Aussie creation works just as well on Kiwi trout. It takes its name from a spotted caddis moth found in the Brindabella Ranges.

BLACK FLY · WAITAKI SEDGE · DAMSEL FLY · GRAEME'S CADDIS · GREEN CADDIS LARVA · BROWN MAYFLY · MUSKRAT · GREEN STONEFLY · PINK ATTRACTOR · COCKSEDGE

Clinton River, Fiordland

Over 80 years ago, Dr Mottram, an English angler-entomologist, fished this remote wilderness river, joyously relating his experiences in the now famous book *Fly Fishing, some new Arts and Mysteries*. In this he lists eight New Zealand mayflies with descriptions and suggested artificial patterns. He ends a chapter on the Clinton . . . "Thus I found Paradise".

Today thousands of walkers each year follow the Clinton on the first two days of their five-day Milford Track experience. This world famous walk is an historic trail between the head of Lake Te Anau and Milford Sound, in the million-hectare Fiordland National Park. The Milford Track must surely be one of the most beautiful, and in parts spectacular, walks in the world. What is amazing is that the Clinton is still a paradise for anglers — the river is full of large wild trout. The gin-clear water and "spookiness" of these fish makes fishing a challenge but they are there and in numbers!

The season opens 1 November and closes 31 May — Milford Track closes early April. Bag limit is three trout but guided walkers can happily practise catch-and-release — magnificent meals are part of the service on the Track.

In his classic book *Trout Stream Insects of New Zealand*, Norman Marsh devotes three chapters to his personal vision of paradise — you guessed it — the Clinton. Two of his flies for the river:

RUBY SPINNER
Norman created this to imitate a mayfly commonly found in the area. Fished on an evening hatch around the Forks area, it often "fools" trout we normally only dream about.

EMERALD BEETLE
Pyronata festiva is a beetle well known to large trout. Norman's best trophy Clinton rainbow was no exception.

RED PEVERIL VARIATION
From Gore fishing-guide, John Hannabus. This double-hackled version was developed by the late Bert Hunt from what is considered to be an old English pattern.

CICADA
Mike Vivier of Te Anau's variation on a theme — useful for the Clinton when naturals are on the wing.

SILKWORM
Another effective Vivier pattern for the area — utilising white ostrich feather.

ZUG BUG
An international nymph with American origins. In size 10, it's an excellent stonefly imitation. Te Anau guide Murray Knowles' favourite for the river.

Garth Coghill of Rotorua is a highly regarded fly tier who enjoys reconstructing historical patterns. He is particularly fascinated by Dr Mottram's — the first recorded imitations of New Zealand mayflies.

MOTTRAM'S BLACK-WINGED BLACK
— spinner & dun
The intrepid doctor's inspired imitation of a large mayfly *Deleatidium lillii*. Originals were tied on the banks of the Clinton with very few materials on hand.

MOTTRAM'S GREAT PEPPER-WINGED OLIVE — spinner & dun
Two more successful patterns of Dr Mottram's — this time representing stages in the life cycle of the spiny gilled mayfly — *Coloburiscus humeralis*.

Diamond Lake, Southern Lakes District

This delightful little lake is situated at the northern end of Lake Wakatipu. The only road access is a pleasant 45-minute drive from Queenstown. From this idyllic spot there are glorious views of the Earnslaw Range, with the Richardson and Cosmos peaks in the distance. It comes as no surprise to find that the property bordering one edge of the lake is called Arcadia Station and the area Paradise. It seems a classical Greek scholar was impressed once too!

Diamond Lake contains brown trout only, which average 1.5 to 2kg, with fish up to 3.6kg taken occasionally. It is open all year round, a recent move which adds much to the lake's attraction. Bag limit is six trout but catch and release is recommended if the lake is to remain a good fishery. Best fly-fishing is between November and February but there is reasonable fishing all year. There is good public access, with casting either from the shore or a small boat.

Ron and Anne Stewart run Kiwistyle Safaris, a fishing and hunting operation based in Glenorchy. Ron is a skilled angler and gamebird hunter. He is admirably complemented by Anne, who combines warm hospitality and great cooking, with flair and style. Their lakeside home offers comfortable and relaxed living in a genuinely friendly back-country atmosphere.

GOLF BALL NYMPHS I & II
If you've ever wondered where those missing golf balls go, this may be one answer! That innovative Christchurch tier John Morton unwinds the latex rubber from golf balls and uses different colours of body under it. Mk I has a pheasant wing case and II is Flashabou backed. John had a great day in Diamond Lake using these.

HAREFLASH
A Morton "dual-purpose" which works well in both running and still water.

DRAGONFLY NYMPH
From Mike Montgomery, also of Christchurch. This fly is best fished weighted. Mike uses an interesting technique — he drops the nymph on the lake bottom and immediately retrieves it at speed for a metre or so, forming a "track" on the bottom. Then a slow retrieve. Trout seem to see the line and follow it!

TADPOLE
Often seen on margins of lakes, tadpoles must appear succulent morsels to trout. Here Mike forms the head close to the eye of the hook to give a more realistic effect.

DAMSEL FLY NYMPH
Dressed lightly with no added weight. Best fished just under the surface in a zig-zag fashion, giving the appearance of a nymph preparing to hatch.

PARACHUTE PEACOCK
Nigel Birt, who guides regularly for Lake Brunner Lodge, tied this highly visible fly. He uses it both on lakes and rivers.

JO-JO JUGGINS
An original Birt creation, named for a friend at the lodge. Reference to a dictionary begs the question — are they still friends? Nigel finds this smelt/Hare & Copper hybrid extremely effective in lakes.

YELLOW HEAD
Inspired by George Gatchell's well-known Burglar patterns, Garth Coghill tied this up to imitate the small forage fish which gather on the edge of lakes. Under water the rabbit fur pulses with life and the tail flicks most enticingly.

GOLF BALL NYMPHS I II

HAREFLASH

DRAGONFLY NYMPH

TADPOLE

DAMSEL FLY NYMPH

PARACHUTE PEACOCK

JO-JO JUGGINS

YELLOW HEAD

Greenstone River, Southern Lakes District

It is a pity more New Zealanders don't experience the awesome beauty of the Fiordland National Park/Southern Lakes region. It is an area brimming with geological, natural, historical and climatic interest. Even the sandflies are impressive!

To anglers the opportunity for true wilderness fly fishing in majestic surroundings is irresistible. Casting to large, visible trout using light tackle is guaranteed to quicken the pulse of even the most hardened angler. To get to most of the action one must be prepared to walk considerable distances or fly in.

Richie and Elaine Bryant run the Greenstone Valley Walk, a commercial operation similar to the Milford Hollyford and Routeburn tracks. It follows an ancient Maori trail through lovely alpine valleys and towering mountain peaks, past sparkling lakes, sweeping beech forests and golden-tussock river plains. All the less pleasant aspects of tramping such as heavy packs, worrying about shelter for the night and the general decision-making required of one in a potentially difficult environment, are taken care of. One is left to enjoy the trip and such luxuries as modern lodges and long hot showers. Richie selects his guides well — they are skilled cooks, full of local knowledge, qualified first aiders and show great consideration to their charges.

There is adequate time to fish on the standard trip in stretches such as the Middle Greenstone, featured here.

Richie Bryant is happy to organise specific fishing trips for groups though. Local guide and well-travelled angler Roy Moss, considers the Middle Greenstone (in November-January) to be one of the world's top dry fly rivers.

Tom Kroos, senior conservation officer, Department of Conservation, Queenstown, says a recent drift-dive survey counted 40 large fish per kilometre in this area — 95% of which were rainbows. The average rainbow taken was 1.9kg with a catch rate of one fish per hour in January. Most were taken on the dry fly with 87% released. Anglers surveyed had an average 18 years' fly-fishing experience. There is a three-fish bag limit but with the Greenstone's delicate and vulnerable balance the voluntary catch and release figures are heartening.

MAYFLY NYMPH
Tied by keen young Christchurch angler Nigel Birt, who in his school holidays is an apprentice guide at Lake Brunner Lodge in Westland. An excellent fish taker.

MOLE FLY
An old English pattern which is deadly on the Greenstone, especially at cicada time. Tied here by Pat O'Keefe, a mainlander who now runs a specialist fishing shop in Rotorua.

BLACK GNAT
Another old-world fly, useful on summer days. Probably taken by the trout for a blowfly (*Diptera* spp.).

M.M. NYMPH
"Marshall's Monstrosity" — named after originator Graeme Marshall (*Stalking Trout*) and designed to imitate emergent insects in the back country. Tied by Nigel Birt.

STENOPERLA PRASINA
Two beautiful representations of this colourful insect — the Green Stonefly. From the innovative vice of Garth Coghill, a regular contributor to *NZ Fisherman* magazine and this book.

HARE LEG HARE'S EAR
Well-known American angler Gary Borger loves to fish in New Zealand, especially the South Island back country. This is an original Borger pattern.

PEVERIL-OF-THE-PEAK
Thought to be an old Derbyshire pattern. Effective when the manuka beetles are on the wing in summer.

HARE AND COPPER
If one was allowed only a single nymph to fish back-country waters this would have to be it. A simple and incredibly successful variation of this fly, tied here by Basil Jackson. Note tuft tied in at the head, suggesting perhaps the emerging wings of a nymph.

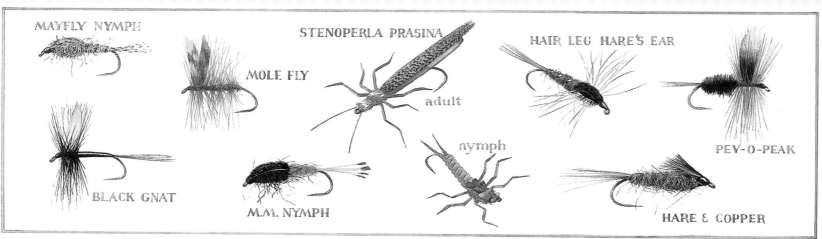

MAYFLY NYMPH

STENOPERLA PRASINA

HAIR LEG HARE'S EAR

MOLE FLY

adult

BLACK GNAT

nymph

PEV-O-PEAK

M.M. NYMPH

HARE & COPPER

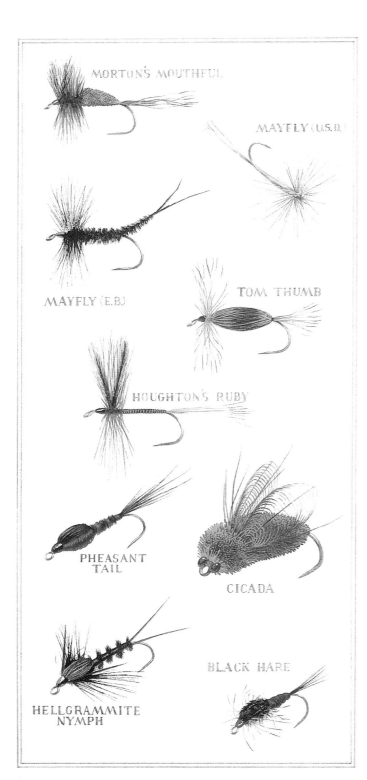

MORTON'S MOUTHFUL

MAYFLY (U.S.D.)

MAYFLY (E.B.)

TOM THUMB

HOUGHTON'S RUBY

PHEASANT TAIL

CICADA

HELLGRAMMITE NYMPH

BLACK HARE

Lochy River, Lake Wakatipu

Rugged mountain ranges tower above this beautiful lake. Several excellent fishing rivers flow into it, one of which is the Lochy — only a short jet boat ride from Queenstown.

Lake Wakatipu itself is habitat for rainbows, browns and even land-locked quinnat salmon. Best fishing around the lake is between November-March.

Roy Moss is a retired Hong Kong policeman who settled in Queenstown. He is a specialist dry fly guide and has a regular clientele of mainly North American anglers. Roy's particular love is the Lochy — he knows every ripple in it and most of the trout too!

We had a glorious autumn day with Roy on this lovely stretch of water. A late mayfly hatch had fantails fluttering furiously. Roy quietly showed us a pair of New Zealand falcons (*Falco novaeseelandiae*) which nested up the valley. Fearless hunters, these beautiful birds of prey are capable of speeds up to 200 kph. It was a magical day . . .

This scene shows the Lochy wending its way down to the lake, with the Remarkables looming in the background. It's typical of many Wakatipu rivers — Greenstone, Caples, Von, Diamond Creek and the Rees. The Lochy is not easily accessible and requires land owner's permission to follow.

MORTON'S MOUTHFUL
A dry fly which works only between mid-December to mid-January. On a No. 12 hook it triggers a spectacular response in trout, especially during the evening rise. From Christchurch tier, John Morton.

UPSIDE-DOWN MAYFLY
Useful pattern on selective trout — giving better presentation of the fly to the fish. A good imitation of our only yellow mayfly *Ameletopsis perscitus*. Tied by Tony Entwistle.

EXTENDED BODY MAYFLY
This beautifully tied fly is the work of Steven Willis from Christchurch. Steven, who has fished since he was four, is a talented fly tier.

TOM THUMB
Once we callously accused this dry fly of "dubious parentage". A letter from Peter Wakefield (International Fly Dressing Corporation, Hong Kong) put us right! It is a Canadian pattern originating in British Columbia. Works exceptionally well on the Lochy, too.

HOUGHTON'S RUBY
Popular dry fly tied to imitate the iron-blue spinner of English streams. Here it resembles *Deleatidium vernale*.

PHEASANT TAIL NYMPH
A New Zealand favourite. Weighted here with fine copper wire. Tied by Basil Jackson.

CICADA
One of the best cicada patterns we've seen. Created by Bronwyn Wilson from dyed deer hair and tied-back cock hackle wings. A succulent morsel for a trout, indeed.

HELLGRAMMITE NYMPH
Bronwyn's version of the U.S. nymph. Floss and ostrich body. Hawk quill tail and feelers. Synthetic seal's fur thorax with black coal hackle, ribbed through it twice.

BLACK HARE
Represents most small mayfly species and fishes well all season. Most effective in size 14, slightly weighted.

Eglinton River, Te Anau

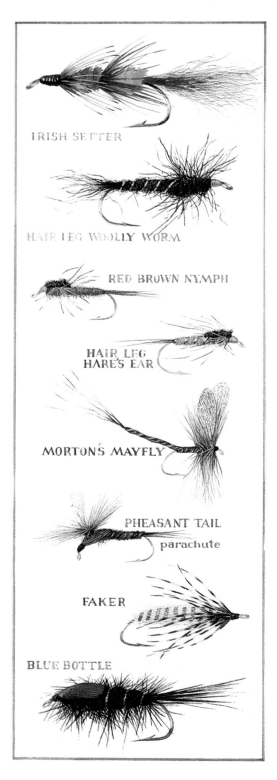

IRISH SETTER

HAIR LEG WOOLLY WORM

RED BROWN NYMPH

HAIR LEG HARE'S EAR

MORTON'S MAYFLY

PHEASANT TAIL
parachute

FAKER

BLUE BOTTLE

This crystal-clear river runs out of Lake Gunn and into Lake Te Anau. The gravel bottom is easily waded at most times. The fish population comprises rainbows and browns in equal proportions. An average fish is around 2kg with the impetuous rainbow easier to tempt than his wily cousin.

Access is easy — featured is the lower gorge area where an angler could wade contentedly for miles in beautiful seclusion. Season is 1 November to 31 May. A three-fish bag limit is in place with fly fishing only permitted. Insect life abounds on this river.

Trevor Halford, an experienced local fly-fishing guide knows and loves the Eglinton. One of his favourite patterns is:

IRISH SETTER
An attractive lure useful both in river and lake situations. Orange and green chenille body, furnace hackle and squirrel tail.

Gary Borger is an Associate Professor of Botany at the University of Wisconsin. He is equally distinguished in fly-fishing circles — as a writer, video film producer and authority on the art. Gary, a regular visitor to New Zealand, has produced a superb video entitled *South Island Sampler*. It shows his love for our waters, our fishing and our country. He says he couldn't imagine fishing the South Island without these three flies and has taken many New Zealand trout on them.

HARE LEG WOOLLY WORM
Originated to imitate larvae of aquatic beetles and moths and the larvae of fishflies, alderflies and dobsonflies, Gary finds it a great match for our dobsonfly larvae.

RED BROWN NYMPH
A great imitation of many mayfly nymphs.

HARE LEG HARE'S EAR
Another Borger favourite (sorry Gary, favorite) for imitating mayfly nymphs.

John Morton is one of New Zealand's most innovative tiers and has two patterns here for the Eglinton.

MORTON'S MAYFLY
Extended body flies are beautiful but the difficulty is in making them durable and yet flexible. This fly evolved and has been a winner for March hatches especially.

PHEASANT TAIL (PARACHUTE)
This is the dry-fly version of the popular Pheasant Tail nymph and it works best November to January. Hook shank is bent slightly, tail end weighted with lead wire so it hangs down in the surface film — with the thorax providing the above-surface profile of the emerging *Deleatidium vernale*.

Another regular is Martin Langlands. Two Langlands creations for the Eglinton:

FAKER
This excellent nymph's success is due mainly to the swannundaze segmented body, translucent camel-hair dubbing (giving impression of gills) and soft hackle representing legs.

BLUE BOTTLE
Another successful pattern. Black rabbit dubbing and metallic blue peacock wing case. Useful in peak summer conditions when the natural is around.

Pomahaka River, West Otago

The township of Gore has proclaimed itself the "Brown Trout Capital of the World"! The good citizens (or more correctly the Gore Lions Club) erected an impressive nine metre high, one-tonne, brown trout statue to prove their point. Bob Jones, well known property magnate and angler, performed the unveiling. He made the point that Gore, despite the severe rural recession, was being positive in its optimistic outlook on other options for the district's future. With several world class trout rivers close to the town the tourist potential has to be good.

One of these is the Pomahaka — a snow-fed river rising in the Umbrella Mountains and flowing some 135 km through the West Otago and Popotunoa districts on its way to a confluence with the mighty Clutha. The upper Pomahaka (above Switzers Bridge) offers the angler large brown trout and lovely rolling scenery. The water is usually clear, flowing over a clean gravel and boulder bottom. Access to most of the river is excellent. Large pools and riffles hold some of the best brown trout to be found in this country. These range in size from 1 to 4.5 kg with an average (best in Otago) of around 2.3 kg. The season opens 1 October and closes at the end of April.

There is a four-fish bag limit on the upper section of the Pomahaka. Public access is easy at Wilden Bridge; elsewhere landowners' permission should be obtained.

GREEN STONEFLY
Neil McDonald, a Tapanui angler and fly tier, has an extensive knowledge of the area too. His nymph here imitates the *Stenoperla prasina*, one of many mayflies encountered on the Pomahaka.

POMAHAKA RED
As the name suggests this is a dry fly originating locally. Neil has noticed that the local trout take in large numbers of small black spiders, house flies and blowflies during the summer months. He thinks that this fly is taken for these. Also used as a searching pattern when rises are not evident.

MAC'S CADDIS
Very effective at dusk or in the evening. Tied on a 2x long nymph hook to simulate the correct proportions for a caddis fly.

McROBBIE
Tied especially by Neil to assist a local angler who was having trouble seeing flies on the water. The fluorescent green floss body solved the problem. Very useful in broken water.

THE BANDIT
A lifelike sedge pupa pattern from Keith Collins. Works well on fish in shallower water — using an induced take ("Leisenring lift"). Body is of olive-brown and medium-brown acetate flosses. Thorax is grey-brown hare's fur with guard hairs removed. Wingcase is constructed from hen pheasant centre tail-feather fibres. The hackle is of mallard duck breast-feather fibres, tied in as a beard.

IRON MAIDEN
An original pattern from Nigel Birt, a young Christchurch angler and tier, who spends most school holidays as an apprentice fishing guide for Lake Brunner Lodge. He created this dry fly specially for New Zealand conditions, inspired by an American pattern. Its speckled wing and slight body (with small hump behind the wing) are, Nigel feels, the secrets to its success.

BLOWFLY
Richard Abrams, an American who has fished the Gore area extensively, finds this Al Troth pattern works well there.

CICADA
Another Al Troth fly used by Richard. It is devastatingly attractive to large trout. Sometimes fish will rise from the depths of a deep pool to slurp in a drowning cicada.

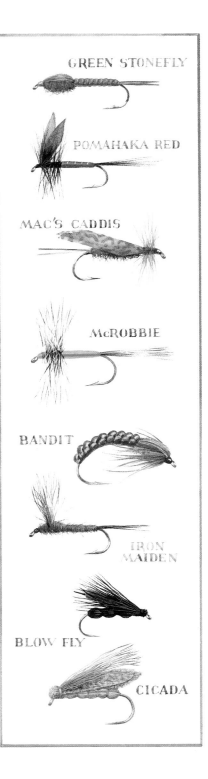

GREEN STONEFLY

POMAHAKA RED

MAC'S CADDIS

McROBBIE

BANDIT

IRON MAIDEN

BLOW FLY

CICADA

Waipahi River, South Otago

The Waipahi originates in tussock country 30 km west of Balclutha and has long had a reputation as one of the finest fly fishing rivers in the country. It runs mainly through rolling sheep and cattle country. Originally this would have been pure tussock land; the conversion to pasture has meant the Waipahi discolours more quickly and for longer than it would have previously. Despite man's "improvements" it is still a river which can absorb high angling pressure and yet give the skilful angler excellent results. Access in most places is easy.

The Waipahi opens on 1 October and the first two months provide superb dry fly fishing, with prolific fly hatches. The weather is often bleak at this time but an angler's hardiness and perseverence is well rewarded. Fishing is far more difficult in the warmer months but in March/April the Waipahi comes into its own again with both insect and fish life in abundance. It closes at the end of April.

A rocky bottom with undercut banks is perfect water for the scrappy 1-2kg brown trout. Main food sources are mayfly, caddis, snails and koura.

The late Bill McLay was a regular Waipahi angler. A retired Dunedin engineer, sometime guide, regular speaker on piscatorial matters, conservationist and member of the Acclimatisation Society Council — Bill had a passionate interest in preserving and improving the water quality of our rivers. A founder member of Dunedin's Fly Flingers and Stream Bashers Club, Bill was also an accomplished fly tier. He tied this series to represent a range of flies in the genus *Deliatidium*. The two most commonly found crawling nymphs in the Waipahi are *D. vernale* and *myzobranchia*.

HARELUG NYMPH
Bill found this to be the best all-round representation of crawling nymphs.

POLYDUB NYMPH
Dressed with polydub body material — floats on the skin of the water representing the nymph just prior to emerging.

NO HACKLE DUN AND PARA DUN
Both tied with polydub body material. The Para Dun has deer hair wings. Both float well and represent the emerging dun.

CONVENTIONAL WET AND DRY
Traditional dressings of wet and dry dun. Commonly used patterns for *Deleatidium* are Dad's Favourite and Blue Dan.

SPENT SPINNER
This pattern should be dressed lightly yet float well. The wings here are of slips of organza, tied in and then the cross weave removed. Body of polydub or quill. This fly is deadly when there is a good rise.

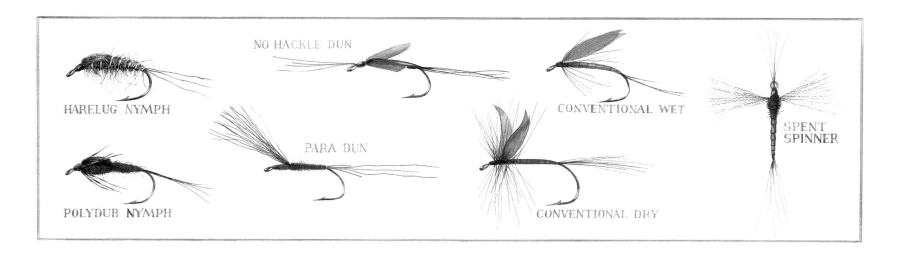

This page is dedicated to the memory of Bill McLay — a true angler and gentleman.

WOOLLY CADDIS

MATAURA RED

WILLOW GRUB

DAD'S FAVOURITE

PHEASANT TAIL

GREY DARTER

BLUE DUN

BULMAN'S FAVOURITE

Mataura River, Southland

It must be a very monastic angler who has not heard of the Mataura River. To many, including a regular caravan of overseas anglers, it is the epitome of the ideal trout stream. Throughout its 160-kilometre journey it is well stocked with hard-fighting hrown trout. Insect life is abundant with the *Deleatidium* species being predominant. Trout feed ravenously on these insects and often ignore the angler — even at close quarters. This phenomenon is called the "Mad Mataura Rise". Although not as dramatic over the last few years, due perhaps to disastrous floods, there are, fortunately, signs of a come-back.

Norman Marsh knows and loves the Mataura. We are indebted to Norman for taking the time to show us "his" river and tie up a selection of his favourite flies.

WOOLLY CADDIS
A Marsh original created to imitate the *Hydropsyche* caddis. Works well early in the season. Thorax: black floss. Body: grey-blue underfur of hare. Plus a sparse tuft of ginger hen hackle fibres tied at the extreme end of the hook. On a 14 or 16 caddis hook.

MATAURA RED
Norman's imitation of a spent *Deleatidium* spinner. Darker when wet. Thorax: grey hare underfur. Body: fawn hare fur over crimson silk. Wings: slip of cream polywing (tied spent). Tail: a few strong red cock fibres. In sizes 16 or 18.

WILLOW GRUB
Simple but effective imitation of the Sawfly larva, much loved by trout in summer. Body: pale primrose floss silk. When wet this darkens nicely to the rich yellow of the natural. In sizes 16 or 18.

DAD'S FAVOURITE
One of Southland's most popular dry flies. It owes its existence to an error in the tie of a traditional English pattern (Dark Red Quill). Body: stripped peacock herl quill. Hackle: brown or finger cock. Wings: grey mallard quill. Tail: brown cock fibres. In sizes 14 or 16.

PHEASANT TAIL NYMPH
A successful English pattern which is an excellent representation of the *Deleatidium vernale* and *myzobranchia* brown nymphs. Body: fine copper wire and pheasant tail fibres. Wing case and tail: pheasant tail fibres. In sizes 16 or 14.

GREY DARTER
A tried and true pattern imitating the *Nesameletus* spp. fast swimming nymphs. Thorax and abdomen: sandy-grey hare fur. Wing case: grey mallard wing fibres. Legs: partridge hackle. Tail: short tufted partridge hackle fibres. Ribbing: dark copper wire. In size 14.

BLUE DUN
A pattern over 300 years old. Effective when both *Deleanitium vernale* and *D.lillii* are about. Body: yellow tying thread dubbed with hare underfur. Hackle: brown dun cock. Wings: dark starling. Tail: blue dun cock.

BULMAN'S FAVOURITE
Noel Bulman is the manager of a leading Invercargill sports store and another keen Mataura man. About 18 years ago, whilst guiding American visitors on the river, he created this fly or, as he says, it "evolved". Semi-palmered ginger hackle; cinnamon silk body mallard quill, grey mallard quill wings. Best when the water is slightly discoloured and in size 16.

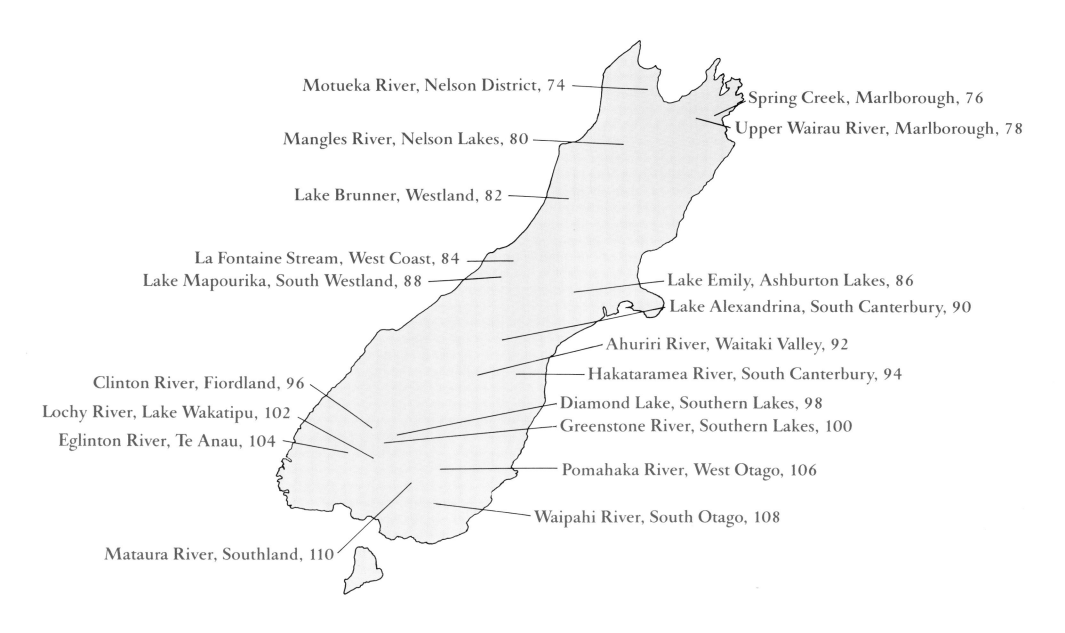

Motueka River, Nelson District, 74

Spring Creek, Marlborough, 76

Upper Wairau River, Marlborough, 78

Mangles River, Nelson Lakes, 80

Lake Brunner, Westland, 82

La Fontaine Stream, West Coast, 84

Lake Emily, Ashburton Lakes, 86

Lake Mapourika, South Westland, 88

Lake Alexandrina, South Canterbury, 90

Ahuriri River, Waitaki Valley, 92

Hakataramea River, South Canterbury, 94

Clinton River, Fiordland, 96

Diamond Lake, Southern Lakes, 98

Lochy River, Lake Wakatipu, 102

Greenstone River, Southern Lakes, 100

Eglinton River, Te Anau, 104

Pomahaka River, West Otago, 106

Waipahi River, South Otago, 108

Mataura River, Southland, 110

Waipapa River, Northland, 18

McLaren Lake, Tauranga District, 20

Waiteti Stream Mouth, Lake Rotorua, 26

Lake Rotoiti, Rotorua Lakes, 24

Lake Ototoa, South Kaipara Peninsula, 16

Te Wairoa Stream Mouth, Lake Tarawera, 28

Lake Rerewhakaiitu, Rotorua District, 32

Lake Aniwhenua, Bay of Plenty, 30

Waipa River, Waikato-King Country, 22

Waitahanui River, Lake Taupo, 40

Whanganui Bay, Lake Taupo, 42

Rangitaiki River, Rotorua District, 34

Tongariro River Delta, Lake Taupo, 46

Ruakituri River, East Coast, 36

Pouto Pool, Tongariro River, Turangi, 48

Waiau River, East Coast, 38

Stony River, Taranaki, 50

Upper Mohaka River, Kaimanawa Ranges, 44

Maunganui-o-teao River, Central North Island, 52

Ngaruroro River, Hawkes Bay, 54

Mangawhero River, Wanganui District, 58

Tukituki River, Hawkes Bay, 56

Rangitikei River, Central North Island, 60

Mangatainoka River, near Pahiatua, 62

Otaki River, Wellington District, 68

Waiohine River, Wairarapa, 64

Hutt River, Wellington, 70

Ruamahanga River, Wairarapa, 66

Wainuiomata River, Wellington, 72

NEW ZEALAND WATERS OPEN
ALL YEAR (1991)

Bay of Islands, Hobson, Mangonui, Whangaroa, Whangarei Districts — all waters.

Auckland District — all lakes except Parkinson's and specified areas of various rivers.

Central North Island Conservancy District — Lakes Taupo, Rotorua, Okareka, Aniwhenua, Maraetai, Whakamaru, Ohakuri, Atiamuri, Aratiatia up to Huka Falls, Rotokura and Dry Lake, Ohakune and specified areas of numerous rivers within the district. Tongariro River (downstream of the point where it is joined by the Whitikau Stream). Southern shoreline of Lake Rotoiti between Ruato and Hinehopu. Shoreline fly fishing between landmarks at Te Koutu Point and west of Okataina Lodge and Lake Okataina and between landmarks at the Te Wairoa Landing, Lake Tarawera.

Hawkes Bay District — Lakes Opowehi, Tutira and specified areas of various rivers.

Wellington District — all coastal dune lakes, Lakes Namu Namu, Wairarapa and the upper Kourarua Dam, the Hutt, Kauwhatau, Moawhango, Ohau, Oroua, Pohangina, Ruamahanga, Tauherenikau, Tiraumea, Turakina, Waikanae, Waingawa and Waiohine Rivers and specified areas of various other rivers.

Marlborough and Nelson Districts — the Cobb Reservoir and specified rivers within the district.

West Coast and Westland Districts — Lakes Brunner, Mahinapua, Ianthe, and the Big Waitaha, Big Wanganui, Cook, Fox, Karangarua, Waiho, Whataroa, Buller, Grey, Karamea, Little Wanganui, Mokihinui and Nile Rivers and specified areas of various other rivers with the district.

North Canterbury District — the Heathcote River and a specified area of the Avon River.

South Canterbury and Waitaki Valley Districts — the Pukaki-Ohau hydro canal.

Otago District — Butcher's, Conroy's, Phoenix and Poolburn Dams. Lakes Onslow, Waipori and the Tomahawk Lagoon and specified areas of other lakes and rivers within the district, except that fishing is prohibited during the first weekend in May (opening of the game season).

Southern Lakes Conservancy District — Lakes Hawea, Wanaka (& Outlet), Wakatipu, Diamond, Hayes, Te Anau, Manapouri, Monowai, Hauroko, Poteriteri and Hakapoua.

Hawea River, Clutha River (portion), Kawarau River and Lower Waiau River. Plus all waters draining to the Tasman Sea between Makawhio and Puysegur Points. But excluding certain specified portions of these open season waters — refer local licence.

NEW ZEALAND TROUT FISHING CALENDAR

October, November and December — Spring and early summer.
A good time to fish in New Zealand, although the weather can be unkind. By the end of this period all waters are open for trout fishing. Prolific smelting in Lake Taupo and Rotorua lakes with excellent harling and fly fishing, particularly in Taupo's Western Bays and the Tongariro river mouth. Excellent early season fishing in the Southern Lakes area.

January and February — Mid summer.
Great fishing throughout the South Island — the best fly fishing is available now. Rotorua and Taupo lakes fishing well to streamer flies especially near stream mouths. Lake harling is good too, particularly mornings and evenings. Good fly fishing on small streams at Rotorua and Taupo. Best time for fly-in wilderness fly fishing throughout the country.

March and April — Late summer.
Weather usually remains settled. Smelting finished in lakes, but good stream mouth fishing. Harling is still good on most lakes. Both North and South Island streams fishing well to dry fly and nymph.

May and June — Autumn and early winter.
Some good fly fishing at stream mouths, particularly on Lakes Tarawera, Rotoiti and Okataina for trophy trout. Excellent fly fishing in the Tongariro and other Taupo tributaries. Excellent late season streamer fishing at river mouths flowing into the Southern Lakes chain.

July, August and September — Mid winter.
Coldest time of the year, often with frosts. Spawning runs in Taupo tributaries are at their best. Harling on Lake Taupo and specified lakes in Rotorua area. Some shoreline fly fishing opportunities on specified Rotorua lakes. Some good winter fishing in the Southern Lake District.

COPPER DAMSEL NYMPH

LIMITING YOUR KILL

by Tony Orman

GREENWELL'S GLORY DARK

It's a paradox in trout fishing that while basically the angler is the hunter and the trout the prey, in a mature person the desire to kill is secondary to the challenge and the sport.

Trout Unlimited, the American trout fishers' organisation, has a motto of "Don't kill your limit, limit your kill". It neatly puts into a nutshell the philosophy behind the sport of trout fishing.

A trout is frequently too valuable to kill. Such is the case in wilderness trout rivers where the size of the trout and aesthetics such as scenery, solitude and space make it a quality experience. Such fishing can be preserved by the "limit your kill" philosophy. Low bag limits may have merit, so could 'catch-and-release', but how do you police such regulations? It is impossible.

When it comes down to reality, limiting your kill or releasing trout is over to attitude.

As Aldo Leopold in *Sand County Almanac* put it, the peculiar thing in fish and game sports is that the ethic is not governed by a gallery to applaud or condemn the play. Rather it is the individual's conscience which is the gallery and the final judge.

Yet there should be no stigma attached to killing trout in some circumstances if the fish is "needed". Some rivers can stand an annual harvest. Other rivers have a fine, delicate balance which almost demands "catch-and-release".

It can be argued that some catch-and-release adherents may be effective in killing trout and needlessly wasting them as the fish which they have subjected to severe stress and build-up of lactic acid, dies. If you intend to release a trout, play it with care yet speed so that stress is minimised. As sporting as it might seem to use ultra-light gear, carrying the concept to extremes may result in released fish dying. Use the maximum strength of nylon cast you can within the needs of presentation.

New Zealanders have been brought up with a kill syndrome. It manifested itself into outdoor sports of two or three decades ago when individuals overkilled whether with rod, rifle or gun. Some may argue otherwise, but the influence of visiting Americans has seen the belated introduction of sporting attitudes to the fishing world.

New Zealand anglers are realising that sportsfish are a finite resource to be appreciated, nurtured and respected. Limiting your kill is a practical application of that philosophy.

CATCH AND RELEASE

Contributed by Dr John Hayes, Fisheries Research Centre, MAFFish, Rotorua.

BLUE DUN

It is doubtful whether any trout water in New Zealand is fished heavily enough to require catch-and-release to conserve its entire stock. This extreme management option is necessary in some North American waters which have "zero-creel" policies. However, in our own country there are some fisheries, mainly in headwaters, for which conservation of a large trophy fish by this method might be desirable.

The sensitivity of large headwater fish to quite moderate fishing pressure was noted as far back as 1932 by Edward Percival. Unfortunately, not much progress has been made in understanding and managing these fisheries since that time. Even if the need for conservation measures in some of these fisheries is established, the success of catch-and-release regulations would depend on the good-will of anglers. By their very nature headwater wilderness areas are impossible to police.

Moving away from these managerial headaches . . . how do caught-and-released fish respond to their repeated excursions to the river bank? The answer to that question seems to be that they respond remarkably well. Studies in the USA have found that mortality of trout released after capture with artificial fly or lure is generally less than five percent. In one fishery, individual trout were caught an average of 10 times over a 50-day period!

The type of gear used doesn't seem to matter too much to the trout, except that fish returned after swallowing natural baits may have very high mortalities — up to 40 percent. There seems to be no difference between mortalities of fish caught on artificial lures with treble hooks, and flies with barbed and barbless hooks. The mortality rate following release can increase at higher temperatures, and when fish are played for excessive periods. So if you intend to release trout, play them carefully yet with speed, to minimise stress, especially in summer.

"The prick of a hook, a few minutes of dancing on the end of a line, the gentle handling of skilful release, will not kill a creature designed to survice the batterings of a dangerous lifetime."
— from *Fisherman's Spring* by Roderick Haig-Brown

THE MANNERS OF FISHING

Contributed by the Internal Affairs Department.

Fish that won't bite, unsuspected snags, wind in the wrong quarter; these are some of the natural hazards that make fishing what it is. The unnatural hazard, however, the inconsiderate action of another angler, is another matter. Nothing is more likely to spoil a day's fishing.

There are few fishermen who would deliberately want to spoil another's sport, so we can take it that in most instances if someone offends against our ideals of fishing courtesy it is through inexperience, inattention or even excitement perhaps. If someone transgresses then we need a little patience. A gentle word perhaps — give the chap the benefit of the doubt. After all, you can't expect him to notice there's something wrong just by your compressed lips, white knuckles and whiplash casts.

BLACK GNAT

What would we tell the inexperienced, someone like our own son perhaps, who has ventured from the solitude of a quiet stream to share a pool on a big river with some very intimidating gentlemen?

We could say firstly that fishermen respect the early bird and that someone already fishing should be allowed to continue without interference, and we don't usurp his position if he leaves it temporarily. The early bird should not become a hog however, and unduly monopolise a piece of water. Be careful who you call a hog though, he might not be aware that anyone else is interested in the same water.

If one or more fishermen are already fishing a pool you may join in but please, not in the water someone is just going to fish. If the pool is being fished downstream start upstream of those already fishing. If they're fishing upstream, start downstream of them. And *please* don't commit the most heinous crime of fishing a pool downstream such as in the case of dry fly and nymphing streams. Similarly don't start fishing upstream towards someone already fishing downstream in waters like the Tongariro.

When you hook a fish you'll appreciate the courtesy of other anglers in giving you room to play it and will promptly do the same for them when the occasion arises.

RED UPRIGHT

Excessive wading or walking close to the river bank will disturb fish unecessarily so you'll keep back from the water when changing fishing places, particularly in the vicinity of another angler. When lake fishing at small stream mouths you'll keep back in line with others and let fish come in to everyone. Don't wade out and ''hog'' the rip.

Be sure when casting that your back cast won't menace other fishermen or innocent bystanders, and don't hang around where you'll restrict someone else's casting.

If you don't know and observe the local fishing regulations, summarised on the back of your licence, you won't be popular with other anglers. You can't enjoy a sport when some of the participants are cheating.

A lot of pleasure of fishing is in the environment. Help to keep it pleasant by cleaning up litter left by less thoughtful people than yourself.

ANGLERS' RIGHT OF ENTRY

A 20-metre public right of way follows both banks of most popular fishing rivers, and to the water's edge surrounding most of the lakes. However, to reach the rivers and lakes, access across privately-owned land is often required. A fishing licence does not confer legal rights of entry, but this is usually accorded almost everywhere in the country, providing — of course — permission is sought.

LOVE'S LURE

WADING SAFETY

Wading is enjoyable and widely practised. It can also be hazardous and treated lightly — DANGEROUS. Never stride out confidently — always move with a short shuffle from one point to another. When wading streams and rivers, keep one leg upstream of the other; and a wading stick is a useful added safety device — it can be used to feel one's way and in an emergency it becomes a third 'leg' as a balance point. A good wading stick will be chest height in length, have a metal bottom tip and be equipped with a loop/hook for suspension off body gear when not in use.

Loose fitting chest waders are not necessarily dangerous when water filled but when you've got them on in these conditions, don't attempt to climb up out of the water. Chest waders normally trap a considerable amount of air and they can be life savers — particularly when a belt is tightened around the upper torso. If you go under when wearing such waders *don't panic*. Simply *turn onto your back* and your bouyant waders will lift your feet to the surface — *keep your legs straight* once they're up; your nose and mouth will be out of the water. *Go with the current*, hand paddling toward the shore. In a river proceed feet first. Try it out in a swimming pool — you may be pleasantly surprised — and it may later avoid panic when you are in real difficulty.

WATER BOATMAN

EARLY BROWN

ACKNOWLEDGEMENTS

PEOPLE WHO TIED THE FLIES

1987 (in order of the Calendar): Clark Reid, Basil Jackson, Martin Langlands, John Morton, Steve Willis, Norm Marsh, Bronwyn Wilson, Tony Entwistle, Ron Mackay, Hugh McDowell, Ray Punter, Roy Marshall, Geoff Woodhouse, Nigel Wood, Doug Wakelin, Maru Maniapoto, Geoff Gower, Alan Hall, Graeme Webb, Garth Coghill and Cliff Dixon.

1988: David Dannefaerd, Noel Baty, Gary Kemsley, Mark Sherburn, Peter Shutt, Barry Stone, John Hayes, Barry Vowles, the late Bruno Kemball, Bronwyn Wilson, George Gatchell, Steve Willis, Herb Spannagl, Tony Hayes, Cliff Henderson, Basil Jackson, Garth Coghill, Roy McKenzie, Keith Collins, Martin Langlands, Bruce Robertson, Bill McLay, Trevor Halford, Gary Borger, John Morton and Alan Waites.

1989: Martin Langlands, John Morton, Steve Willis, Jim Greeks, John McDowell, Mike Weddell, Jack Dennis, Garth Coghill, Mark Sherburn, Tom Kemper, Phil Steck, Jack MacKenzie, Hugh McDowell, Ray Punter, Gary Kemsley, Tony Fetch, George Gatchell, Pat & Helen O'Keefe, John Kent, Ali Thompson, Keith Collins, Tony Hayes, Bob Christie, Frank Harwood, Basil Jackson, Roy Cotter, Doug Allen, Malcolm Shield, Bill McLay, Tony Entwistle, Peter Carty, David Moate, Ron Mackay, Nigel Birt and Gary Borger.

1990: Frank Schlosser, Steve Willis, Peter Schasching, John Morton, Keith Simpson, Gary Borger, Brian Hussey, Dave Mabin, Geoff Robinson, Al Troth, Tony Orman, S/Ldr A.G. Smith, Norman Marsh, Bill Kirk, Lee Chin Choon Tan, Wayne Harter, Garth Coghill, Pat O'Keefe, Helen O'Keefe, Pat Swift, David Syme, Hugh McDowell, Ken Duncan, Basil Jackson, Barry Birchall, Gerald Wilson, Tony Hayes, Martin Langlands, Bill McLay, Mike Montgomery, Andrew Altman, Neil McDonald, Keith Collins, Nigel Birt, Jim Ackerley, Derek Smitheram, Jim Tonkin, Neville Adams and Robert Wright.

1991: Harry Brown, Chris Bright, Richard le Mesurier, Ali Thompson, Lee Chin Choon Tan, Mike Montgomery, James Douglas, Mike Gopperth, Martin Langlands, Norman Marsh, John Hannabus, Mike Vivier, Garth Coghill, Tony Orman, the late Syd Peterken, Allan Rush, Basil Jackson, Brian Batson, Pat Swift, Pat O'Keefe, Michelle Batson, Max Sheffield, Maureen Butler, Hugh McDowell, Daphne Gatchell, Bronwyn Wilson, George Gatchell, the late "Budge" Hintz, Carrynne Scarlett-Rise, Even Rise, Geir Kjensmo, Rolf Ahlkvist, Steve Willis, John Morton, Nigel Birt, Graeme Warren, Barry Cooke, Graeme Hughes, Frank Schlosser, Noel Thomas, Chris Hole, Ken Duncan, Dennis Ward and Lindsay Lyons.

DAD'S FAVOURITE

PEOPLE WHO HELPED IN OTHER WAYS

1987 (in order of the Calendar): Mike Manion (South Rakaia Hotel), John Grainger (Newmans Air, Rotorua), Jocelyn and Roy Moss (Queenstown), Ann and Graham Rive (Halfway Bay Station, Lake Wakatipu), Sharon Entwistle (St. Arnaud), Jack Bell (Rotorua), Mike Harrison (McCoy & Thomas Sports, Whangarei), Sandie and Ian Page (Tahere), Mark Davenport (Waikato Valley Authority, Hamilton), Phyll and Graeme Marx (Otorohanga), Steve Thomas (Otorohanga), Steve Snedden (Taupo), Melva and Alan Atkins (Lake Waikaremoana), Peter Pegram (Wairoa), Jean Marsh (Invercargill), Noel Bulman (Outdoor World, Invercargill), Dave Stack (Rotorua) and Dick Marquand (Queenstown).

1988: Dudley Smith (Russell), Anne and Hugh Canning (Waipapa), Elaine Shutt (Timaru), Ellen Vowles and Allan Jesperson (Paeroa, Margaret Coutts (Tongariro River Lodge), Di and Peter Gifford (Hastings), Phillipa and Russ Ballard (Wellington), Mike Slee, Chris Burr and Steve Smith (Wellington), Marion van der Goes and Ray Grubb (Lake Brunner Lodge), Mary and Mike Browne (Christchurch), Helen Leach (Dunedin), Pam Halford and Bill Jarvie (Te Anau), Jocelyn and Roy Moss (Queenstown), Margaret and Don McMillan (Wanganui), Newmans Rentals (Auckland), John Grainger (Rotorua) and Ansett New Zealand, Auckland.

ADAMS

1989: Simon Rowland-Jones (Christchurch), Steve Smith (Wellington), Myrna and Stan Peterson (Franz Josef), Lesley MacKenzie (Mangaweka), Ursula and John Brown (Ngongotaha), Janice and Brian Batson (Raupunga), Cliff Dixon and Alan McKnight

(Wairoa), Bob Jones (Wellington), Di and Peter Gifford (Waitetoko), Walker family (Huapai), Dave McLellan (Milford), Dave Hartley (Mt Wellington), Balt Bender (Onehunga), Dianne and Larry Cotter (Pahiatua), Dawn and Cliff Fergus (Pahiatua), Keith Fergus (Pahiatua), Sharon and Nicky Entwistle (St Arnaud), Elaine and Richie Bryant (Queenstown), Liz Dickinson, Jos McLean, Nic Scott, Jenny Grimmett and Tom Kroos (all of Queenstown), Jocelyn and Roy Moss (Queenstown), Maureen Davis (Mount Cook Airline, Rotorua), Greg Shanaghan (Air New Zealand, Rotorua) and Lynn Huhtala (Newmans Rentals, Auckland).

1990: Wink Mabin (Hastings), Rosemary and Graham Sutton (Timara Lodge, Blenheim), Dick Abrams (Chicago, USA), Glen & Stan Davenport (Doone Cottage, Motueka Valley)Graeme Marshall(Motueka Valley), John Keedwell (Carterton), Steve Smith (Wellington), Anne and Hugh Canning (Waipapa), Noel Birchall (Kaikohe), Jennifer and Punch Wilson (Taupo), John Parsons (Taupo), Jim Dodgshun (Palmerson), Helen Leach and Mary and Mike Browne (Inch Cottage), Olga and Bert Harvey (Gore), John Hannabus (Gore), Ron Stewart (Glenorchy), Greg Shanaghan (Air New Zealand), Kay Kosar (Mount Cook Airline) and Newmans Rentals (Auckland).

1991: Steve Mason (Taumarunui), Jim Gosman (National Park), Liz and Peter Fitchett (Rotorua), Daphne Douglas (Culverden), Dr John Hayes (MAFFish, Christchurch), Robert Romauch, Mihi and Warwick Chinnery and Dave Grant (Milford Track), Ray Punter (Rotorua), Bridget Woodrow (Plimmerton), Steve Smith (Wellington), Jennifer Wilson (Taupo), Janice Batson ('Waikohe', Raupunga), Bill Butler (Rotorua), Cara Hintz (Taupo), Jan Jolley (Albany), Peter Davies (Rotorua), Mary, Mandy and Mike Browne (Christchurch), Anne and Ron Stewart (Glenorchy), DenizeWarren (Kurow), Jenni Duncan (Tauranga), and Lynn and Rewi Tapsell ('Mockingbird Hill', Harihari).

BLACK & GREY NYMPH

PUBLICATIONS WE FOUND USEFUL

Ackerley, Jim. *The Ashburton Lakes*. Self published, 1986.
Bain and Greig. *Fishing Guide to the Tongariro River*. Wetland Press, 1983.
Draper, Keith. *Trout Flies in New Zealand*. Reed Methuen, 1984.
Forrester, Rex. *Trout Fishing in New Zealand*. Whitcoulls, 1987.
Hammond, Bryn. *The New Zealand Encyclopedia of Fly Fishing*. Halcyon Press, 1988.
Hill, Les & Marshall, Graeme. *Stalking Trout*. Seto/Halcyon Publishing 1985.
Kemsley, Gary. *Taupo Fishing Guide*. Lithographic Services, 1983.
Kent, John (Dr). *North Island Trout Fishing Guide*. Heinemann Reed, 1989.
McDowell, Hugh. *New Zealand Fly Tying*. Reed Methuen, 1984.
Marsh, Norman. *Trout Stream Insects of New Zealand*. Millwood Press, 1985.
NZ Fisherman. Vantage Publications. Various back issues.
NZ Sportfishing Marketing Group Booklet. *Land of Fishing Legends*. 1984.
Parsons, John. *Deceiving Trout*. Seto/Halcyon Publishing, 1988.
Rotorua Trout Fishing Guide. Rotorua Anglers' Association, 1985.
Shutt, Peter. *Fishing in the South Island*. P. Shutt, 1986.
Weddell, Mike. *Ten of the Best New Zealand Trout Flies*. John McIndoe, 1987.
Whitlock, Dave. *Guide to Aquatic Trout Foods*. Winchester Press, 1982.

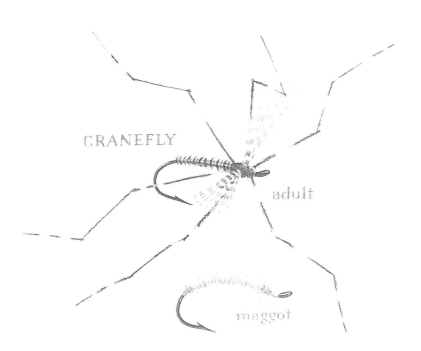

CRANEFLY

adult

maggot

INDEX OF FLIES

adult

nymph   ORANGE MAYFLY

Index of Places Illustrated